Data Management for Professionals

by Bryan Lewis

Chairman, Yankee Computer Services, Inc.
Yorktown Heights, New York

D1279459

Data Management
for
Professionals

by Bryan Lewis

ASHTON·TATE ■

10150 W. Jefferson Blvd.
Culver City, CA 90230
(213) 204-5570

Cover design: D.A. Gray
Cover photography: Stanley Gainsforth
Illustrations: Paul Winters
Editor: Robert Hoffman
Associate Editor: John Leddy
Production Manager/Designer: Thomas Clark
Publications Director: Jane Mellin

To Jan, Carolee, and Jeff
My own Mrs. O'Hara, Scarlett, and Rhett

Table of Contents

Chapter One

Introduction

You're a professional. You take pride in your work. Whatever your profession—whether you're an attorney, a medical specialist, a general practitioner, a dentist, or a pharmacist—your work is judged on its merit, and your name is judged with it. You've invested years in education and experience to get where you are today.

That's the image that most often springs to mind when we hear the word "professional." But there's another meaning: *someone who works for a living*. A non-amateur. Someone engaged in an occupation for pay. Whatever your reasons were for choosing your particular specialty, you have to receive a positive net income sooner or later!

There's the rub. You've had to learn to be a businessman in order to prosper in your chosen profession. For many of you, that's been an unwelcome experience. If you're a typical family doctor, for example, you're already working 70 to 80 hours a week on your practice, but you can't quite keep up with all the new developments in medicine, or meet with your colleagues as often as you'd like. You really don't have the time to track every insurance company or patient that owes you money, or to learn the latest government regulations, or to redesign your

ASHTON·TATE ■

accounting procedures—*even though all those things would probably improve your bottom line*!

Often, the solution to this time-versus-money tradeoff is to hire other specialists to take care of the business aspects. You might hire an office manager to look after your billing and payroll and to order supplies. In place of (or even in addition to) the office manager, you might let an outside billing service handle the paperwork and collection chores. You probably rely on a receptionist, an accountant, and a lawyer for help in other areas. Of course, there are drawbacks to all that delegation. It costs money, and you pick up new responsibilities in the area of people management.

I know some of you professionals are protesting already. Yes, some of you really do handle everything yourself. You order your own supplies, prepare your own income tax returns, and write the bills to your clients. More power to you! You're the entrepreneurial type, and you get a lot of satisfaction from being your own boss.

Unfortunately it's becoming more and more difficult to stay in control of all the details, simply because there are more details than ever before. Here are a few recent developments that require you to divert attention from your profession, or else place yourself at a competitive disadvantage:

> •There are more government regulations than ever before. You might have to file detailed reports on your sales of controlled drugs, or on minority employment statistics. The tax laws alone are at an all-time high of complexity: FICA, unemployment insurance, investment credits, sales tax; plus an increased emphasis on accurate record-keeping and audit trails.

> •There are more rules from your own professional societies and independent testing organizations. Often the societies have imposed these rules on themselves to forestall government intervention.

ASHTON·TATE ■

•Your liabilities are greater than ever before. The courts have taken the attitude that you must foresee all possible effects of your actions, and document your preparations for them.

•Because of the escalating costs of liability insurance and record-keeping, and the high investment required to get started, some professionals are joining together to share the expenses. Medical, dental, and legal group offices are becoming more common. These "groups" are likely to aim for a high-volume business, often borrowing from the marketing techniques of retail stores: locating in shopping malls, selling generic brands, advertising prices.

•New technical developments are occurring at an ever-increasing rate. For you that means having to learn more new techniques and gadgets tomorrow than today. Most of the new technology involves either small computers or telephone communications such as: electronic submission of insurance and Medicaid claims; on-line databases (that is, large collections of information you can search through via a telephone connection); computers in your own office; computer-assisted diagnosis and interpretation.

Reading that list is depressing, isn't it? You may be thinking the days of the hardy, self-sufficient individual are gone forever.[1]

Wrong! There's no reason to close up shop. The rules of the game are just a little different now. If you're willing to learn and to change a little, you can fight back by taking advantage of some of that same technology. In the past, you probably thought automation was only for manufacturing industries, or for the really information-intensive businesses like investment firms and banks. That was true, but now those industries have automated so much that the

ASHTON·TATE ■

"professional office" has been left behind. *You* are now the industry that can benefit most from automation. But why now? Because it's only in the last few years that computers and storage devices have become powerful enough and cheap enough to come within the reach of small businesses and professionals.

We're all familiar with the decreasing cost curve for electronic components, if only from observing the price of calculators. If we were to sketch the history of cost versus capability, we'd see something like the graph shown in Figure 1.

The curve has moved down and to the right with time. The year 1981 is often cited as the beginning of a new era. That was when several important developments (16-bit microprocessors, small Winchester disk drives, and memory circuits capable of storing 64,000 bits of information) all became available.

That's why you're hearing more about computers than ever before. Computers are powerful enough and inexpensive enough now to be affordable in an office like yours. But let's not miss the point by getting lost in technical discussions. Being affordable is not the same thing as being a good investment. What will such a machine do for you?

Here are several areas in which you can expect to see benefits—ways in which you can make yourself more competitive.

Faster cash flow. With a good automated office system, you can quit worrying about invoices falling through the cracks. Your system can make sure you know what's owed to you and who's being forgetful.

Less paperwork. Paperwork is the most obvious indicator of all those new regulations and rules and liabilities we talked about. But it's not a new problem. Read this description of a businessman written 65 years ago, and see if anything sounds familiar to you:

> Papers, letters, bits of half-finished jobs
> were scattered on his desk. People came
> in at all hours and dumped more

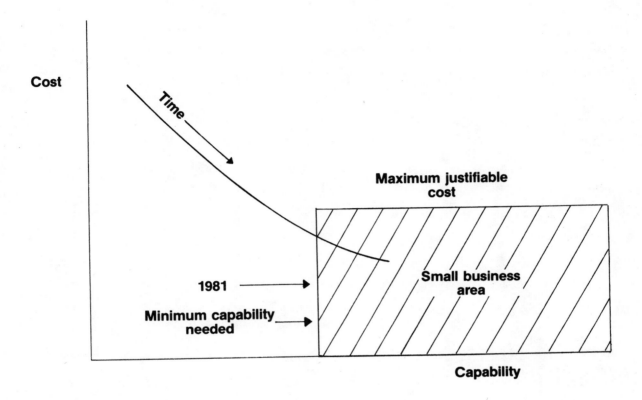

Figure 1. Decreasing cost curve for computer systems

papers on his desk. Elbow room was
out of the question, so the man had to
be a contortionist to do his work.
When a certain paper was wanted, the
only way to get it was to search
through the desk. Hunting for lost arti-
cles took so much time that the man
didn't have a chance to make a living.
He never caught up with his work.
When a client or customer wanted
immediate action or information, every-
body in the office was in consternation.
Among the total impossibilities of life
was an exact knowledge of how the
business was going.[2]

That scene has been reenacted many times, but its days
are finally numbered. Reduction of paperwork is the easiest to visualize advantage of a computer. Most of you
would feel the difference immediately if you automated the
printing of all those repetitive forms—bills of materials,
insurance claims, statements, appointment reminders.

A more thorough understanding of your business. You'll be
able to analyze which procedures or cases or customers
have been the most rewarding to you. Maybe there are
aspects of your business you don't particularly enjoy, but
they're bringing you a good income (you think). A systematic set of records will allow you to determine for sure
whether they're worthwhile, and whether you can justify
hiring an associate or helper to take them over.

Better security. This is one of those benefits you hope
you'll never need. If you ever have to show detailed
records to an auditor, or if you're victimized by burglary
or fire, you're in a lot better position with a computerized
office than with shoeboxes full of receipts. Computerized
records are easier to duplicate, to protect, and to restore
on a moment's notice. One reason is simply size; a small
box of magnetic disks (smaller than this book) can contain
the essential information from a room full of filing cabinets.

ASHTON·TATE ■

Better contact with your clients. Obviously you'll have more time to spend with your clients if all the other wonderful things we're talking about here come true. But more time isn't the only reason your image with your customers will improve. A computer can make it practical to send personalized letters to some or all of your clients to remind them of upcoming appointments, to wish them a happy birthday, or to notify them of new tax laws, or medical treatments, or whatever you think they should be kept aware of.

We'll be exploring these benefits and others in greater detail; but now, at least, you have an idea of why small computers are attracting so much attention. There's a real revolution going on, one that will eventually affect the way you do business just as much as the automobile or the telephone did. And it's only beginning to gather steam. In the kinds of professional offices we're discussing here, about ten percent are using computers now. In the next eight years, that usage is projected to rise to 50 percent.[3]

But in this book I am not trying to convince you to run out and buy a computer today. The things you want to do might not be practical yet; that is, they might not be doable at a reasonable speed on a computer of a size you can afford. Or they might be possible but no one has thought to do them yet. Better still, you may be able to get most of the benefits without investing in a computer just by streamlining your office procedures and being more systematic with the data you already have on your clients. The purpose of this book is to let you know what's commonly available, and to get you thinking of possibilities.

The next chapter lays the foundation for our study by describing the concept of data management, and why a computer is needed to do it. Chapter Three will show you *how* a computer (or a human, for that matter) accomplishes the chores we'll be talking about—by *outlining*[4] exactly what is meant by such terms as "accounts receivable management" and "profitability analysis."

PREVIEW

ASHTON·TATE ■

After we've established what the common functions are and how they work, individual chapters will be devoted to specific professions: doctor, dentist, pharmacist, and lawyer. Each of these chapters will refer to the common procedures outlined in Chapter Three where necessary. (For instance, almost all professionals have a need for accounts receivable management.) This will allow a more thorough discussion of the details peculiar to each profession, plus a few real-life case histories.

At that point you should be able to judge whether you need a computer for your office. If owning your own seems feasible, the last chapter will tell you what kind of performance (speed and capacity) to expect for how much money and how to make the investment wisely.

Notes

1. If any of you are pessimistic enough to believe that George Orwell was right on target in his evocative book *1984*, you're wrong literally as well as figuratively. He envisioned a world in which all information was controlled exclusively by the state. He didn't predict the widespread ownership of personal computing and communication devices. How would you like to be the government official with the job of controlling all the information contained in and passed between a million small computers?
2. Written in 1919 by Edward Earle Purington and reprinted in *How to Become Financially Successful by Owning your Own Business*, by Albert J. Lowry, ©1981, Simon an Schuster, New York.
3. From the report "Vertical Markets for Microcomputer Software" by International Resource Development Inc., quoted in *Computer Retailing*, March, 1983.
4. Note well my choice of the word "outlining." When you start to write a report or a book, you probably put together an outline first—just the main points, written in short, plain English sentence fragments, with some semblance of organization. That's how I'll present the procedures in Chapter Three. No computer programs in this book!

ASHTON·TATE ■

Chapter Two

What's It Good For?

In this book we'll be discussing what I call the *management of data*, just one type of computer application. It doesn't include all uses—not even the ones most people associate with computers. The mythical man on the street, if you can find him, still pictures a computer as a number-crunching machine. As Joseph Weizenbaum explained,

> "Many people know that a computer can compare their names as imprinted on credit cards with names somehow stored inside the computer. Yet most people believe computers are fundamentally machines that can do arithmetic on a grand scale, i.e., that they are merely very fast automatic desk calculators. Although this belief is defensible on strictly formal grounds, it is much more useful to recognize that a computer is fundamentally a symbol manipulator. Among the symbols it can manipulate are some that humans, and in a certain sense even computers, interpret as numbers. Still, most

computers spend much, even most, of
their time doing nonnumerical work."[1]

The first distinguishing characteristic of data management is the relative unimportance of numerical calculations. Many of the applications in this book can be achieved even if calculations are not allowed. Indeed, I have achieved good results in the past with data management systems which have had exactly that deficiency; they wouldn't add 2 and 2, and made no pretensions to the contrary. They were, however, quite fast at symbol manipulation: finding names, alphabetizing them, printing, and moving text around. Although numbers were involved, zip codes for instance, they were treated as just another symbol.[2]

Narrowing our definition even further, we will not include word processing. That's the manipulation of words and not numbers, but the management aspect is missing. Word processors do not, in general, make decisions based on what a particular word is. They do not keep some words and discard others without very specific instructions from you.

In the simplest terms, data management is the entry and automatic retrieval of routine tidbits of information like names, addresses, and eye color. The information is usually textual in nature, although numbers aren't ruled out (like zip codes). Each individual piece is usually small and well-defined. The automatic retrieval includes operations like discarding some tidbits while simply ignoring others, making a decision on another group (such as, send a letter if the account is overdue, not otherwise), and rearranging (sorting) all of it into a new order. If you start with a large enough number of tidbits and perform several steps like these, especially the decision-making step, the final conclusion can be quite surprising—even though no single piece of information is new to you.

Operations like these may strike you as simple, not requiring a computer. Each piece of information *is* simple. It's the *volume*, the number of pieces, that makes it hard to grasp. Psychologists tell us that human beings are not good at processing large streams of new data and information. The most we can hold in short-term memory is six or seven pieces.

Take the phone directory as a familiar example of a database.[3] The information is simple enough: name, address, phone number. But what if someone gave you a number and asked you to find the name? That analogy can be extended to the information generated every day by your business: invoices, date of treatment, age, and so on. They're all simple in concept, but what if someone asked you to mail a gift to every client with a birthday in August, provided he had paid his bills on time for the past six months? With your present manual methods you'd probably say it's too much work, even if you liked the idea for its marketing value.

I'm compelled to introduce a few terms here (five to be exact), so you and I will be talking the same language throughout the rest of the book. They're not really all that different from words you use every day in your office. Let's pretend you're in your office, talking to your assistant about looking up some information in your file cabinets. Your discussion might go something like this:

"I want to send reminders to every
client who hasn't been in for a year.
Sift through the 'active client' file cabinet. Pull out every folder and check the
date of the last visit. That should go
pretty fast. Remember we always wrote
the last visit in the upper right corner
of the folder."

That same request between two programmers is:

"In the active-client database, find every
record in which the contents of the
last-visit-date field is over a year ago."

You might wonder why programmers have to invent new words. Why database instead of file? Why record in place of folder? What's a field? The reason is the same one that prompts the rest of you professionals to create words

THE INEVITABLE DEFINITIONS

peculiar to your specialty—precision of meaning. That's
the importance of all the following definitions.

Data is any information, whether it's number or text or
just a check mark in a box. Thus, it's a generic term in
the same sense that "food" is a generic term. "Text" is a
kind of data; "vegetables" are a kind of food. But data
doesn't mean just any haphazard collection of information.
The word connotes a rigid, predefined format. If you're
dealing with a collection of data, you know in advance the
type of each piece (text, numbers), its maximum length
(20 letters long, or ten digits long), and where it is in
relation to all the other data. Think of filling out an
income tax form—last name here, first name there, dollars
down here with the cents on the right of the vertical
line—that's data.[4]

A *field* is the slot reserved for an individual piece of
data, with predefined length and position. It's the box on
the form that allows you 20 letters of space. In our
conversation above, "last-visit-date" was a field. Other
examples are last name, phone number, and balance due.
The information contained in the field is the smallest
tidbit of data defined, one item.

Any given field will always be located at the same place.
In our conversation, the last-visit-date was always in the
upper right corner of the folder. Note well: The name of
the field ("last-visit-date") and its type and length also are
constant. Only the *contents* of the field change, depending
upon which folder we're holding at the moment.

A *record* is the grouping of data relating to one case,
one account, or one client. The fields are the same in
each grouping, but their contents change. A record corresponds to one whole file folder. One whole income tax
form is a record describing you; someone else's is another
record.

You may be disturbed by the statement, "The fields are
the same in each grouping." That's not the way it is in
your file cabinets! Some clients have two phone numbers
while others have only one, to give a trivial example.
You've been handling that by squeezing the extra phone

number into the margin. That's exactly the difference I want to point out. If your file cabinets were to be replaced by a computer, you'd have to decide in advance whether to provide slots for two phone numbers. No squeezing allowed.[5]

You might also be disturbed by the fact that a record has such a wide scope; it can contain the data for something as small as a transaction or something as large as an entire folder. The important characteristic is that the record's structure is constant: every record in the file has the same fields in the same order.[6]

A *database* is the whole file cabinet. All the income tax forms in the country make up a database. The important characteristic is that all records in the database have the same structure, the same field names, lengths, and arrangement.

A personal address book is a good example of a database. (See Figure 1.) This particular address book's layout clearly separates the individual fields (name, address, etc.). The complete entry for one person is a record. The entire book is a database. But if you pencil notes in the margins ("This person sleeps during the day, call in the evening."), then it's not a database any more. You've added information that isn't predefined, that doesn't fit into a field. You've made it hard to retrieve that information by any systematic method. That doesn't mean you can't add that kind of information; simply place an extra field called "Comments" on every record. That way it will always be in the same place and easily retrievable.

Finally, a *data manager* is what I call the system that carries out the entering, arranging, and retrieving of the data. The term is deliberately ambiguous. It might be a group of clerks using a common filing cabinet, or a computer, or even an outside company that provides data processing services. The only requirement is a systematic, predefined method of storing the data.

As for what you can do with a data manager, that's what the rest of the book is about. But remember that no one can give you a complete list. Some applications just aren't thought of until people use the new technology in everyday situations. After you get used to having a data manager in your office, you'll think of your own new applications.

If you want to get accustomed to this expanded way of viewing your business's "information potential," you can start now by remembering all those brainstorms you get, like the "birthdays in August" example. If you're an efficient businessman, you've probably trained yourself to ignore most of those ideas; they're impractical right now, too much paperwork, too much overhead. In the future, make a list of those ideas. After a while you'll see a pattern of kinds of information with value—kinds you should be collecting like gold coins.

I find it helpful to consider first where the information comes from. There are two main sources:

Personal data—things your clients tell you about themselves such as name, address, and age.

Transaction data—facts you know directly from your business with them, from the history of all past transactions.

Obviously you have to remember a client's name, address, and phone number. This is personal data, the basic information you need to identify a client. It is sufficient for constructing a database; remember the address book example. You don't have to know much more in the way of personal data to realize the benefits of client list management. The important information comes next.

To the personal data you're going to add transaction data. Every service or procedure you provide will be added to the database, one record at a time. Each item of business—document, payment, consultation—will be another record. The exact nature of a transaction (the fields within the record) will depend on your profession and your own style. For example, if you're an attorney your records usually concentrate on time spent with a

YOUR HOMEGROWN DATABASE

Name			
Street			
City		State	
Zip Code	Area Code	Prefix	No.

Name			
Street			
City		State	
Zip Code	Area Code	Prefix	No.

Name			
Street			
City		State	
Zip Code	Area Code	Prefix	No

Name			
Street			
City		State	
Zip Code	Area Code	Prefix	No.

Name			
Street			
City		State	
Zip Code	Area Code	Prefix	No.

Name			
Street			
City		State	
Zip Code	Area Code	Prefix	No.

Name			
Street			
City		State	
Zip Code	Area Code	Prefix	No.

Figure 1. Personal address book

client and the reason. If you've ever used a "pegboard" timekeeping system you already know the fields:

- Date of service.
- Attorney's initials (in multiple-attorney firms).
- Client's name or account number. (This has to be there so you'll know who the transaction is for, even though the name is personal data and already stored. A computer programmer might call this the *link* to the personal data.)
- Name of case or matter involved.
- Service performed (consultation, document preparation, court appearance, etc., in words or abbreviated code).
- Time spent (usually in hours and tenths of hours).
- Money (dollars paid by client, a positive amount, or spent on the client's behalf or otherwise billable, a negative amount).

Typical entries in the file (that is, typical records) are:

Date	By	Client	Matter	Service	Time	Money
9/04/83	JBL	John Doe	Will	Conference	2.0	-150.00
9/05/83	JBL	John Doe	Will	Document		-50.00
9/30/83		John Doe	Payment			200.00

Notice that I'm using the same record structure for all of the transactions, despite differences in the natures of the transactions. The first record is a charge based on an hourly rate. The second comes from a fixed fee for document preparation. The third is a payment.

Most likely, this is not how you are keeping your records now. For one thing, you probably just enter your hours and let your assistant calculate the charges. Similarly, your assistant takes care of payments received. But this is how the records should look after all the information is completed, and it's the right way to think of it for our purposes. The primary reason for using the same structure for all transactions is to facilitate the retrieval of information later. If you ever want to find out which clients pay their bills on time (as we'll see in the section on accounts receivable), you'll be glad you kept the charges and payments in a single database.

For a doctor or dentist, the important fields might be:
- Date of procedure.
- Doctor initials or number (if more than one producer).
- Patient's name or account number.
- Diagnosis (usually using standard ICDA codes).
- Procedure performed (in words, abbreviations, or codes such as those standardized by the ADA, ICDA, or CPT).
- Money (charge or payment).

I've arranged the fields in the same order as the attorney's to make the similarity obvious. Unlike lawyers, most doctors are not overly concerned with time spent, since they base their charges on a per-procedure basis. The notable exceptions are psychiatrists, psychologists, chiropractors, and others who provide therapy or consultation—services which aren't easily split into discrete procedures.

A pharmacist would want to remember:
- Date.
- Pharmacist's initials.
- Client's name.
- Drug prescribed.
- Strength.
- Quantity.
- Prescribing doctor's name.
- Money charged (usually broken down into the cost of the drug and the fee for the prescription).
- Date of expiration or refill.

CUSTOM FIELDS

No matter what your profession, chances are you'll want to add a few more items to the fundamental ones we just

ASHTON·TATE ■

listed. For personal data, you might care about your client's age, especially if it has a bearing on the services, prescriptions, or advice you give. (A patient's allergies or preferences for anesthesia may be important.) If you really care about catering to your customers' preferences, don't forget what time of day they would like their appointments, and whether they want their pills in child-proof bottles.

For your daily transactions, you might want to keep track of kind of payment: cash, check, credit card, insurance. Finally, you might assign some code of your own to classify each transaction by segment of your business. For example, it might not be obvious from an attorney's time sheet what kind of case was involved. An extra code of "M" for marital cases, "R" for real estate, and so on might lay the groundwork for some very informative research into profitability.

If you don't *like* working on contested marital cases, and your research shows that they don't bring in their fair share of dollars, then quit doing them or hire an assistant. Even better, raise your rates for contested marital work, which will have the combined effect of reducing the number of such cases and raising their profitability. There's no law that all of your hours have to be billed at the same rate, especially if you have a computer to worry about the multiplication.

By now, you should realize that the kind of information you will collect is not restricted in scope. The best way to decide what you want to collect is to determine first what questions you will want to ask. But we're getting ahead of ourselves; the next chapter talks about how to phrase the questions and what you should be thinking about.

The important thing to realize from this section is that your business, if given a chance, will slowly build its own homegrown database. So, if the word "database" has always brought to your mind a nightmare vision of you and your staff entering thousands of obscure ten digit numbers into a computer, now is the time to change your mind. The data is whatever your business is already

ASHTON·TATE ■

producing and you enter it a little at a time, as it's generated. After a year or so, you will have a real asset—a database you could not buy at any price—based on your kinds of clients, your kinds of services, and your local area. With the help of a computer, you will be able to get quick analyses of that data.

Notes

1. From *Computer Power and Human Reason*, by Joseph Weizenbaum. W.H. Freeman and Company, San Francisco, 1976.

2. By convention, the symbol "4" is less than the symbol "A" (i.e., lower in an arbitrarily agreed-upon pecking order), which was in turn less than "Z." It's true that the convention still regarded a "1" as less than a "2" but it just didn't matter. Whether a "1" is half as much as a "2" is a pointless question, like asking, "Is a stick figure half as much as a dollar sign?"

   The non-programmers among you may be thinking that the convention is some obscure code designed solely to intimidate the average person. I did not have to tell you that a "Z" is less than an "A." The convention is called the ASCII code (pronounced ask-key), for American Standard Code for Information Interchange, and it's undoubtedly the most widely-used code in the history of mankind.

3. If you'd like more of an introduction to the design and use of databases, you can refer to the best-selling book *Everyman's Database Primer* by Robert A. Byers, published by Ashton-Tate.

4. This is the appropriate time for me to clarify one small point of usage, in case there are any other perfectionists out there who are writhing in agony from that last paragraph. I use "data" as either singular or plural. Now hold on—I studied Latin, and I know "data" is properly plural. I reminded people of the proper usage for years, which achieved nothing but a reputation for being boring. I've given up; everyone uses data as a numberless noun.

   As a result, the singular form, "datum," has just about vanished. It could still be a useful word (meaning a single item within the collection of data, the contents of a field), but no one uses it.

5. Don't worry. If you forget to allow for two phone numbers at the outset, you haven't committed a fatal error. You don't have to throw your computerized file cabinet out the window and start from scratch. You can go back and add the extra field when you think of it. The point is that you do have to provide a well-defined slot for all information before it can be added, and all records will have the same fields. In this case, all records will have lines for two numbers, even though you won't need both in many cases.

6. A good analogy is the atom. When I was in grade school, the atom was defined as "the smallest indivisible unit of matter." We now know that the atom is itself made up of smaller particles, but that doesn't destroy its significance. It's still the basic building block that gets repeated over and over to make up matter. But not all atoms are the same; an atom of copper is different than an atom of iron.

   A record is similar. It's the basic building block. Yes, it's made up of smaller particles—the fields. Yes, a transaction record is different from a patient record. But a record is still the repeating unit that makes up a file.

   This analogy isn't perfect. Real matter always has a few impurity atoms; there are a few copper atoms in every piece of iron, but the disturbance isn't usually noticeable. Not so for a database. Every record must have the same structure!

ASHTON·TATE ■

Chapter Three

How Does Your Office Work?

Pretend for a moment that you've just hired a new clerk, someone who has absolutely no experience with office procedures. (If that's a little hard for you to imagine, try this: In a moment of generosity at your favorite niece's high school graduation last week, you agreed to give her a chance in the business world.) You want the new clerk to feel useful from the start, but you know you won't have much time to spend with her during the day, so you conceive the excellent idea of giving her a detailed description of all your routines. Since (1) you understand all your own procedures thoroughly, (2) you don't want to leave anything to chance, and (3) you're naturally a very methodical person, the final product is a masterpiece. You spend your whole weekend on it, ending up with a one inch thick looseleaf binder, a real textbook on how to run a professional office.

Let's say you send birthday cards to your clients once a month. The procedure for your new clerk might look like:

Birthday Card Procedure
Using the client file,
Taking each file folder one at a time:

ASHTON·TATE ■

Look at the birthdate.
If the birthdate falls in the next month from now,
    Write the name and address on an envelope.
Continue until the end of the file.

In real life you'd have more detail than that, depending on how nervous you were about the new clerk. You'd probably say when to carry out this procedure, perhaps the last Friday of every month. You might clarify where to find the birthday entry in each folder: it's in the upper right corner of the blue personal-data card. But that skeleton description is good enough for the purposes of our illustration.

The outline is written in "structured English." By "structured" I mean that it's detailed, with only one simple action or decision to each line, and that it's organized in some standard format. Even the indentation is part of the organization. It makes the outline easier to read and makes it obvious *when* and *if* something is to be done. In this case it's crystal clear that an envelope is only written once per folder, and only if the birthday is during the next month. With this as a guide, your new clerk will have no trouble executing the procedure flawlessly. In more complicated examples, like those we'll cover in this chapter, such an outline can be invaluable.

In fact, I recommend that you take the time to analyze your routines in this way, even if you have no intention of hiring a new employee (or computer) in the near future. Be *sure* to include your office staff—office manager, secretary, and receptionist. Don't try to write it yourself in one lonely sitting as in the above example, and then present it to them as "the way we do things here." If you have a good office staff you probably *won't be able* to spell out your procedures by yourself anyway. The attempt to involve them in the decision-making process may also do wonders for their morale.[1]

Sit down with your office staff. Use a blackboard or easel-sized pad of paper, and for a start, try to list *what* your normal procedures are. I'll bet you will uncover several uncertainties even at this stage. "Why do we do

this?" "Are we doing it often enough or too often?" "That procedure isn't as effective as it could be, because we're not following it up a month later."

In later sessions (of an hour or two each), try to define the procedures in greater detail, until you have a structured English outline of all the important ones. The exercise may greatly raise your office efficiency.

Even in the simple birthday-card procedure, here are a few possible improvements:

- •You'd make a better impression on your clients if you mailed the cards once a week. Fill out the envelopes monthly as before, but band them into bundles to be mailed weekly.

- •You might prefer to send greetings only to clients who aren't delinquent in their payments.

- •When one of the client's folders has no entry for birthdate, make a note to ask them for it when they next come in.

- •If you're a doctor or dentist, maybe you'd prefer to send cards only to your patients who are under 16 years old.

Wait a minute. I can imagine that some of you are reading this with a "Bah, humbug" in the back of your mind. All you see is several hours of wasted effort, with nothing to show for it but a lot of complaints from your staff about how things are run. This exercise cannot *create* complaints, it can only *uncover* them. If you're reluctant to talk to your people, you're only postponing your problems. (Does your office have more than its share of employee turnover? Sick days?)

The wasted-hours objection is short-sighted. Yes, it's probably true that the looseleaf binder full of procedures will sit on the shelf most of the time. Your experienced workers won't need to look at it. But the exercise isn't wasted. It will bring you such benefits as:

- •Getting everyone in the office "speaking the same language," agreeing on how things are

ASHTON·TATE ■

done. This can be a significant benefit (especially if your office suffers from sloppiness) but it's seldom recognized by itself. What usually happens is the implementation of a new system or process, or a reorganization which *forces* everyone to learn the same (new) modus operandi. The newness, not the uniformity, then gets the credit for the improved productivity.

•Generating ideas for improvement, as we just discussed.

•You'll be much better off when you do need to hire a new employee, especially if you have to replace someone who leaves on short notice. Many professional offices are crippled for weeks when a key person leaves, simply because nobody else knows how the person did things.

•Preparing you to talk to a business consultant or data management consultant if you ever decide to. Your homework will already be done. If you buy a computer you'll have clear-cut procedures for the programmer to try to imitate, and to judge the result by. You'll know what aspects of *your* business are unique—the areas a mass-produced program is unlikely to cover, where the consultant will need to customize.

THE WAY MOST OFFICES (AND COMPUTERS) WORK

I want to show you the *logic* of data management; I want to remove the mystique. You can understand how a data manager works if you have only a methodical mind, not a degree in electronics. To accomplish this I'll outline the common procedures performed by a data manager in structured English, just as I recommended for you. When we start talking about a computer performing your office procedures, the detailed outlines become especially valuable. In fact, I had computers in mind when I presented the example of the inexperienced new clerk. A computer is the ultimate in inexperience! It has precisely zero knowledge of how your office works. It must be told everything; more details even than we envisioned in the "birthday card" example. The computer has to be told where to find the file cabinet! It has to be told whether the month or day or year comes first in the birthdate. Nevertheless, the structured English outline is an excellent starting point. It's actually the way many programmers (including myself) start to write a new program, to save ourselves from getting bogged down in a mass of details and loose ends.

I promised in Chapter 1 not to include any computer programs in the book, but here's a very small one. You should see that the structured English outline really isn't that far from how a data management system actually works. A computer equipped with a good data-management language will understand instructions not substantially different from your outlines. Here is an honest-to-goodness program[2] that will look up all the clients you want to see:

Birthday Card Program
```
USE Clients
DO WHILE .NOT. EOF
     IF Birthdate = ThisMonth
          ? Name
          ? Address
          ? City, State, Zip
     ENDIF
     SKIP
ENDDO
```

Now I admit that this presumes a lot of preliminary work. For one thing, someone has to have typed your client data into the computer, so that the data now resides in the file called Clients. And I've glossed over the details of getting the name and address onto the envelope: an extra couple of instructions and some means of feeding envelopes into the printer are required. But once those

ASHTON·TATE ■

preliminaries are done, this program *will* do the job. The similarity to the outline is the important lesson.

That's the last program you'll see here. Now we'll outline the common office procedures in structured English. Don't forget that the outlines are realistic approximations of the way a computer would perform the task. You should also compare the procedures I describe to the way you currently perform the same jobs (if you do).

Of all the uses for a data manager, client list management is the most valuable if you wish to expand your business, to bring in more customers while keeping your old ones. It's also the easiest to understand. For one example, consider a simple mailing list. Let's say you send a newsletter to all your clients—your secretary types each person's name and address on a gummed label for the mailing. You're taking advantage of the list of names you've built up over the years, putting your information to work.

You may be thinking, "Okay, I can see that mailing a newsletter involves a client list, but where's the management? All I've done is copy a list of names from one bunch of papers to another." Not so. Or it shouldn't be so. In the process of typing those labels, your secretary will automatically, almost without thinking about it, filter out certain names. "Here's Mr. Smith, he hasn't seen us in three years. I'll leave him out. And Mrs. Jones here is six months overdue in paying her bill. Skip her."

To really see that there's management required here, think of all the obvious form letters and junk mail you yourself have received. (Multiple copies sent to the same address, special offers to you as a "valued customer" when you haven't bought anything in six years.) You can always tell when a mailing list has been merely copied, without any extra thought or filtering.

The "birthday card" procedure we outlined in the last section is another example of list management. In that case the filtering was more apparent; only the clients with imminent birthdays were to be copied. In other words,

CLIENT LIST MANAGEMENT

ASHTON·TATE ■

there was a different *condition* that had to be met for a name to qualify.

The client list we're talking about is really the home-grown database we introduced in Chapter 2. If you're bothered by the thought of "growing" a database for a year or more before you can really start doing client list management, be reassured that there are other advantages that can be realized in the short run. As we'll see later when we discuss accounting applications, a computer makes a good electronic bookkeeper after only a month of use. It will give you summaries of daily and monthly transactions, and will allow you to call up account information on the video screen quickly.[3] The computer will also serve as a very smart typewriter, by rearranging the transactions you've already entered and then putting them onto a statement, insurance claim, prescription, or any other predefined form.

But here we're talking about longer-term benefits. The real power of an automated data manager is that it allows you to carry out your own data *research*. Now the word "research" has taken on an unfortunate connotation for many people, probably as a result of too many TV commercials. Research does not mean experimentation without goals, direction, or relation to the real economic world. My dictionary defines research as "careful, systematic study." Even the word itself, re-search, is a perfect description of what you'll do with your homegrown database. You'll *search* through the data *again*, through all of those transactions you've seen before.[4]

We've mentioned two simple examples of this kind of research, although they hardly seem worthy of the name— a mailing to all clients and a birthday list. Here are some more sophisticated requests you might ask your data manager:

> **1.** Give me a list of all the wills I've prepared for residents of New York State, and when.

HAND-PICKED DATA

ASHTON·TATE ■

2. Give me a list of all the patients for whom I prescribed the drug Googol (since that drug has just been withdrawn from the market).

3. List all the patients under 40 years old who were prescribed the drug Googol and the drug Yaphrax. Include mailing addresses.

4. Show me all the clients who haven't paid a visit in the past two years.

5. List all the customers taking maintenance drugs for high blood pressure who are overdue for a prescription renewal.

Look through these sample inquiries. Try to name the kinds of information that must be collected in order for the questions to be answered. Computers aren't omniscient, not by a long shot. If you've ever seen any science fiction movies you've undoubtedly heard the metallic voice of a computer or robot saying, "Does not compute," or "Insufficient data"—the computer's version of a shrug. *You* have to decide at the outset what fields you need. For the above list, the important fields are:

1. Service, date, client's address.
2. Medication prescribed.
3. Medication, patient's birthdate, address.
4. Date of service.
5. Medication prescribed, diagnosis, renewal date.

We've left out client names, with the understanding that they always have to be present.

You should try phrasing a few of your own questions, ones that relate to your business. The exercise will establish the pieces of information *you* need to collect, the fields in your database.

Finally, we can return to our original objective: a "structured English" outline of client list management. We've decided upon the kind of data we have to work with, and clarified the kinds of questions we'll want to ask. But how can we come up with a single outline to encompass all those different inquiries? We can't formulate a different outline for every question, no matter how much help our hypothetical new office manager needs!

We can take advantage of the obvious similarity of form in all those inquiries. They all look something like the following:

Standard Recipe For An Inquiry

Show me all *records or pieces of records* for which a specified *condition* holds true.[5]

You will seldom want to see an entire *record*—all the information on a client. A few pieces (fields) from each record, such as name and address, are sufficient.

1. Show me all *names and dates* for which *the service was a will and the client's address is New York.*

2. Show me all *patient names* for whom *medication prescribed was drug Googol.*

3. Show me all *patient names and addresses* for whom *age is less than 40 years and medication was Googol and medication was Yaphrax.*

4. Show me all *names* for whom *the last visit was more than two years ago.*

5. Show me all *names* for whom *the diagnosis is high blood pressure and the renewal date is before today.*

Since we can't know in advance what the specific fields will be, we phrase our request in terms of a condition that must be satisfied. The condition is the entire set of field specifications, no matter how many fields are of interest to us. Here's our outline:

Client List Management Procedure

Using the homegrown database,

Taking each record in turn:

If it satisfies the *condition*,

Print the specified *fields*.

Continue until the end of the file.

That outline may seem trivial, for the complexity is in the condition. When you formulate questions to your data manager, you must take care that you ask for exactly what you want. If you're sloppy in phrasing the question, you might get an answer miles away from what you expected. Take inquiry Number 3 for an example and recall "the parable of the perfect novice office manager": You're

TAKE CARE! YOUR WISH ISN'T NECESSARILY YOUR COMMAND

ASHTON·TATE ■

sitting in your office on Wednesday morning, going through your mail at precisely the correct speed to assure the completion of the chore with the time you have to leave for your golf appointment, thinking how well things seem to be going lately, when the next letter is from a drug manufacturer.

"We feel it is our duty to inform you that certain government tests, as yet unsubstantiated in our own laboratories and as yet neither requiring any change in your treatment nor our distribution plans, have indicated a chance of adverse reactions in patients administered both our drug Googol and another manufacturer's drug Yaphrax," the letter begins in typical everything's-under-control-for-heaven's-sake-don't-anybody-panic style. "The alleged adverse reactions were reported to have a measurable frequency of occurrence only in patients under 40 years of age. We are corresponding with the other manufacturer to find out what they're doing wrong, but ...."

You yell from your office to your perfect novice, "Give me a list of all patients under 40 taking Googol and Yaphrax, and make it snappy!" (Well, of course *you* wouldn't be that brusque, not normally anyway, but for the sake of the illustration we'll intimidate the novice to make sure she doesn't ask exactly what you mean— because that's exactly the way it is with a computer.)

Which of the following lists do you think the novice will bring you?

    A. All under 40 today, who were given *either* Googol *or* Yaphrax at any time.

    B. All under 40 today, given Googol at any time *and* Yaphrax at any time.

    C. All under 40 today, who were given Googol and Yaphrax in the same visit.

    D. All who were under 40 when they were first given Googol *or* Yaphrax.

    E. All who were under 40 when they were first given both Googol *and* Yaphrax.

    F. None of the above.

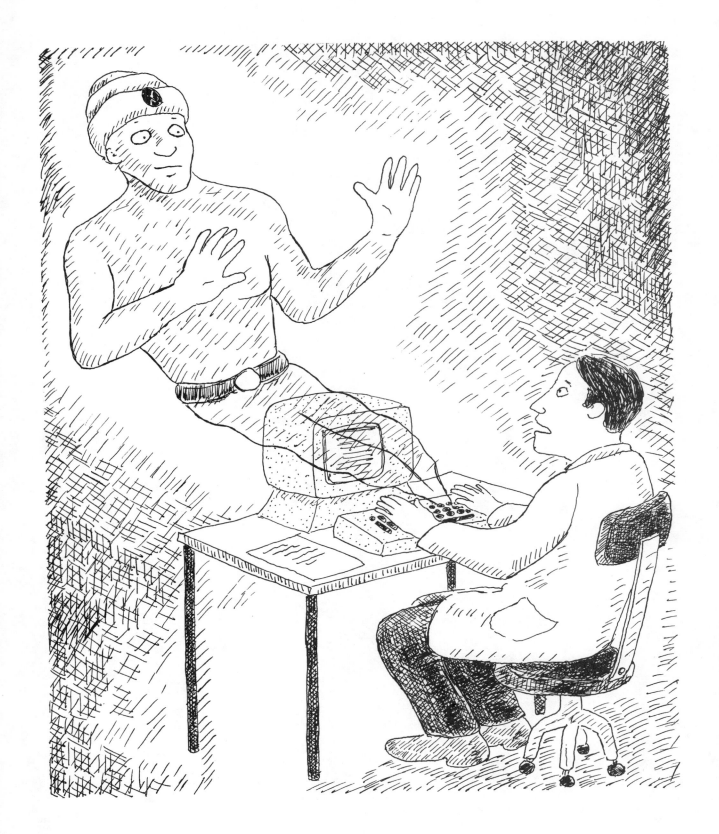

Chances are good that your novice will bring you List A, thinking you want all Googol's and all Yaphrax's (the safest guess). But what you wanted was probably List E. The List A you were given isn't useless, of course, since it contains most of what you want. The only names it's missing are those who turned 40 recently. On the other hand, it contains extra names you didn't want (all the Googol-only's and Yaphrax-only's), but you'll be able to pick out the right ones yourself, won't you? No, you won't, not if the list really contains only names and addresses. You won't have the drug, date, and age data.

How could you have been more precise? Try this question:

> Show me all names and addresses for whom medication was Googol *and* medication was Yaphrax *and* age is less than 40.

The answer will depend on how you designed your database in the beginning. If it has a one-transaction-per-record structure as we've been discussing here, and you've been entering each prescription as a separate transaction, then you'll get nothing—an empty list! For there is no record in the database including two drugs. That's how a computerized data manager obeys your inquiry, by examining each record one by one in obedience to your specified condition. (That was the gist of our trivial outline.)

If the structure is instead one visit per record, with all medications prescribed during the visit included in the record, that same inquiry will give you List C.

Perhaps your initial planning was more thorough than that. You foresaw this difficulty and started a medical history file as well as a transaction file. It contains, in addition to patient name, address, and birthdate, all drugs ever prescribed and all diagnoses ever made. If you apply that last inquiry to this medical history file, you'll get what you want except the age will be today's age. That is, you'll get List B.

Here's a counter-example, using inquiry Number 5: all customers overdue for renewal of blood-pressure medications. In this case you *want* to use your detailed transaction file (one drug per record) to ensure that the renewal date corresponds to the proper medication. If you instead query a *history* file (one with all diagnoses and drugs lumped together), you might end up with people who happened to have had a blood pressure problem some time ago, but are actually overdue for refills of their ulcer medication. They will not be impressed if you mail them a courteous reminder to attend to their blood pressure.

These hypothetical complications are intended to show you the value of planning ahead, but you don't have to be clairvoyant. If you find yourself in this fix, with your data inconveniently arranged for the question you want to ask, you're not lost. You still have three solutions.

1. *Break it down into smaller questions.* A good data manager will let you rearrange or condense your files into new ones. If you want to ask the Googol-and-Yaphrax question and all you have is a transaction database (one drug per record), you should be able to:

•Extract a new database comprised of only those transactions satisfying the combined condition Googol-and-under-40.

•Do the same thing again to get a subset of Yaphrax-and-under-40 transactions.

•List all the names common to both extracted subsets.

2. *Write your own program to handle that class of question.* All data managers have limitations. Instead of blaming yourself for not foreseeing how to design your file, you could justifiably blame the computer for not being flexible enough. We kept our list-management outline simple by working on one record at a time, which inevitably fell short when we started asking global questions like "did anyone ever ...?". If we're willing to get a little more complicated, we can overcome this limitation by designing a new procedure.

As always with a new procedure, begin by outlining how you'd attack it manually:

Look at the transactions for each individual client.
Was Googol ever prescribed before the age of 40?

ASHTON·TATE ■

If not,

that patient doesn't qualify. Skip to the next one.

But if so,

that patient might qualify. Check further:

Was Yaphrax ever prescribed before 40?

If not,

that patient's out. Skip to the next one.

But if so,

you found one! Write down the name and address.

Continue until the end of the file.

You can follow this same step-by-step sequence on a computer, although there's no point to the computer if you have to repeat all the instructions for each client. A good data manager will let you collect such a sequence of commands and give it a name. The computer will then execute the sequence as a unit. What you're actually doing is writing your own program to make up for the lack of a suitable predefined command. The disadvantage to this approach is that it takes more time, thought, and preliminary study than the other methods.

3. *The pragmatist's solution.* You can settle for the quickest and easiest result that contains more information than you need, and then sift through it, by eyeball, to pick out the contained answer. In this example use List A, the one your novice so proudly presented to you, having made sure it includes all the pertinent data—drug prescribed, date, and age. You'll still have your question answered in a much shorter time than with purely manual methods.

ICING ON THE CAKE: PERSONALIZED LETTERS

Some of the examples in the last section looked very much like the beginnings of a mailing. We had the names and addresses of a very specific subset of our clients, just begging to be typed onto envelopes or postcards or gummed labels. Well, that's one way of carrying out the mailing—hand-type the names onto the envelopes.

However, it is extremely easy today to have the computer print the addresses directly onto your mailing materials. Many data management units will print names

ASHTON·TATE ■

and addresses in the usual mailing-label format: name, street, city, state, and zip with one inch allowed per name. If that's good enough for what you want to mail, you can ask for a roll of labels and then just feed it to the printer. You might call this the direct-to-printer method.

A more flexible method is to tell the data manager to save the names and addresses in a new file, consisting of only the names you want in your mailing. To be precise, the new file is saved on one of the computer's magnetic disks, but that technicality isn't particularly important except to distinguish this method from the direct-to-printer method. (This one could be called the intermediate-file method.) Then the set of desired names is available for manipulation by a word processing program, just as if you had typed them directly into the word processor manually. Here's a sample of the most common usage for this capability, the generation of personalized letters.[6]

Pretend you're a lawyer who's just learned about an important revision in the inheritance or estate tax laws of New York State, where you practice. You'd like to inform all the clients for whom you've ever executed a will, that they should call you to discuss the effects of this change, and perhaps revise their wills. You go to your computerized data manager and ask it for a list of the affected clients (that is, you ask question Number One from our earlier examples). You tell the system to list the names and addresses as well as the date of the last revision of the will.

But that list won't ever show up on paper. It's the intermediate file, from which the word processor can print a letter like the one shown in Figure 1.

I've shaded the information that was filled in by the computer's word processor. Any data you extract from your homegrown database can be inserted anywhere in the letter, and the final result will be virtually indistinguishable from a hand-typed letter. Furthermore, the word processor will continue to print customized letters until it has finished your list of selected clients. Of course, you still have to sign the letters yourself.

ASHTON·TATE ■

LAW OFFICES
EDWIN SAMALIN

YORKTOWN OFFICE PARK
2000 MAPLE HILL STREET
P. O. BOX 427
YORKTOWN HEIGHTS, N. Y. 10598

September 7, 1983

Mr. John Doe
123 Main Street
Anywhere, NY   11111

As your attorney and consultant in matters of your estate, I think you should be aware of recent changes in the tax laws of New York State governing inheritances. It is no longer adequate protection to leave your entire estate, or the bulk of your estate after all named items, to your spouse.

Our records show that your will was last reviewed in August, 1980. Feel free to call our office to discuss this matter. If you'd like, I'll be happy to meet with you to explain the effects of the new laws in more detail.

                              Sincerely,

                              E. S. Samolin, Esq.

Figure 1. Personalized form letter

**ACCOUNTS
RECEIVABLE
MANAGEMENT**

Your accounts receivable are all the amounts owed to you—from clients, third parties, insurance companies, or other agencies. The term is derived from the accountant's method of entering all such transactions together under one account heading in the ledger. You can visualize them as filling one page in a large leather-bound ledger book. But you don't have to maintain a complete ledger (which gathers together all your assets and liabilities) in order to keep track of your receivables.

On the contrary, it is quite common for professionals like yourself to keep a close (weekly or monthly) watch on receivables, while paying relatively little attention to other assets and liabilities. By nature, your business is primarily a service business. Your overhead is more or less fixed, consisting of salaries, office rent, and investment in a fairly constant amount of equipment. Your overhead doesn't change much if the number of customers in a given period rises or falls. The only highly variable amount in your overall financial picture, the one that can make the difference between profit and loss, is your receivables. (Pharmacies are an exception. They're not only a service business, they also keep a large inventory. Even so, management of receivables is probably the second most important task for a pharmacy's data manager, after inventory control.)

At the simplest level, good management of accounts receivable (whether manual or mechanized) requires only a meticulous filing system. A box of 3-by-5 index cards, one card for each client, can be a good system if you maintain it conscientiously. You need to riffle through the box once a month to see who's being slow about paying; that is, who hasn't attempted to reduce the balance for more than 60 days (to pick a typical grace period). If the box of cards works well enough so that none of the debts are accidentally forgotten, you have a good system. If none of the debts are allowed to slide past the grace period without your knowledge, you have an excellent system!

ASHTON·TATE ■

The next level of sophistication is a procedure called aging. Aging is a systematic tracking of how old each debt is. You can still use the card box, but there's more labor involved now. After you've riffled through the box, pulling out all the cards with a positive balance on them, you age each account by calculating the precise number of days since each debt was incurred. But that can get extremely messy, since one customer might be responsible for many transactions. "Let's see, here's $100 still owed from May 3, so that's 92 days old. And here's $45 from June 13, which is 51 days old. And here's . . ." It's a lot of work, and you still have to interpret all those precise ages after you've calculated them.

AGING

For most purposes, aging to the nearest month is accurate enough and a lot easier to interpret. Most offices view their accounts in monthly chunks anyway; any finer detail than that is superfluous. To understand how it's done, imagine you're an accountant at the turn of the century, working at one of those massive wooden desks containing dozens of little drawers. Each drawer is fronted with a finger-sized brass handle and a slot for a label. You dedicate five drawers to each of your clients, and label them like this:

J. Doe Unbilled	J. Doe Current	J. Doe Past 30	J. Doe Past 60	J. Doe Past 90

Whenever a new credit transaction comes in, you put the charge slip in the appropriate client's "Unbilled" drawer, to hold it until you get around to sending out your monthly statements. The "Current" drawer contains charges which have been billed but aren't significantly overdue yet. You might prefer to label that drawer as "Past Due Less Than 30 Days."

On the last business day of each month (early in the morning, since it's going to take all day), you sit down to age your accounts and send statements. You move all the charge slips from the "Unbilled" drawer to the "Current" drawer. The "Current" charge slips, if there are any, are

ASHTON·TATE ■

Statement Date   August 31,1983

Amount Due $ 300.00

Account No.   D253

Mr. John Doe
123 Main Street
Hometown, State   12345

AMOUNT PAID $ _____

Please Return This Portion With Your Remittance

Retain This Portion of Statement For Your Records

DATE MO.	DAY	NAME	CODE	DESCRIPTION	
				Balance Forward	$ 200.00
8	15	John Doe	Ph	Physical Exam	45.00
8	15	John Doe	XR	X-ray	15.00
8	15	John Doe	Rx	Prescription	10.00
8	15	John Doe	B	Blood Tests	30.00
					$ 300.00

Current Amount	Amount 30 Days Past Due	Amount 60 Days Past Due	Amt. 90 Days or Over Past Due	PLEASE PAY LAST AMOUNT
100.00	50.00	150.00		

Figure 2. Invoice showing age of outstanding balance

moved to the "Past 30" drawer. Similarly, the old "Past 30" and "Past 60" slips are also moved one drawer. We'll assume that 90 days is as far as you care about; anything that's still unpaid in the "Past 90" drawer will require special handling such as a dunning letter, turning it over to a collection agency, or simply writing it off.

As an illustration, let's say Mr. Doe's drawers already contained several charge slips:

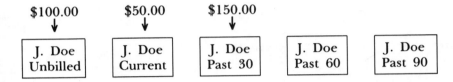

After your aging, the drawers will contain:

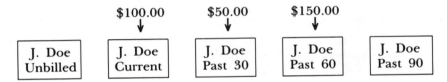

Now you're ready to type up Mr. Doe's statement. It's a straightforward listing of the drawer contents, as shown in Figure 2.

Notice that the unbilled category never shows up on the statement, since by definition there are no unbilled items once the statement goes out. It's an internal category, for housekeeping so to speak.

That's the basic idea behind the management of accounts receivable data. There are several enhancements you might want to add, as we'll see in a moment, but you probably won't add many features as long as you're doing everything manually. Even the simple system we just discussed is a very time-consuming manual chore. To see that, let's outline the procedure in structured English:

Procedure for Accounts Receivable Management
On the last business day of the month,
Using the file of guarantors,[7]

ASHTON·TATE ■

For each guarantor:

    Age the account as follows:

    Add the Past-60 amount to the existing Past-90 total.

    Move the Past-30 amount to Past-60.

    Move the Current amount to Past-30.

    Move the Unbilled amount to Current.

Add the Past-30, -60, and -90 amounts to get a Balance Forward.

Add that to the Current column to get the overall Total.

If the Total is greater than $1.00 (so it's worth the effort):

      Type a statement showing:

        today's date,

        name and address,

        the Balance Forward,

        each individual transaction during the month,

        the Total,

        and an aging summary, showing each subtotal.

    Put the statement in a stack for later mailing.

Continue with the next guarantor until the end of the file.

Put all the file folders back in the cabinet.

For each statement in the typed stack:

    Fold and stuff into a windowed envelope.

    Apply a stamp.

    Put in a second stack for mailing.

Continue till the end of the stack.

Mail the stack.

If Mr. Doe incurs no further charges and makes no payments in the month of September, then the next aging will move all his balances up one drawer, and his statement will look like:

Current	Past 30	Past 60	Past 90
	100.00	50.00	150.00

How much time does all that take? The outline we just drew up can be helpful in estimating how long the whole procedure takes, and in locating the bottlenecks. Some representative figures for a single clerk are:

For all the bookkeeping steps .... 3 minutes
  (opening each folder, adding, aging)
For typing the statement .... 2 minutes
For folding, stuffing and stamping .... 1 minute

Total time per statement .... 6 minutes

That's a fairly good pace. A statement for a new customer or one involving a long series of transactions may require up to 20 minutes, especially if your filing system isn't very methodical (that is, if you have to chase down scattered slips of paper to collect the transactions). We're also including a little overhead to allow for pulling out and refiling the folders, mailing the whole stack, and losing your place every time you're interrupted. So don't delude yourself by holding a stopwatch over your secretary's shoulder to see how fast one statement can be processed.

Thus for each 100 statements you send out, you'll spend 600 minutes or 10 hours. The total is:

6 minutes x 100 statements = 10 hours

if you're sending only 100 statements a month.

With a computerized accounting system, the times are reduced. Exactly how much will depend on how fast the equipment is (especially the disk storage devices and the printer), but we'll analyze that in the last chapter. For now, here are some typical times:

For the bookkeeping steps (looking up
  each guarantor, adding, aging) .... 0.1 minute
For printing the statement .... 0.3 minute
For folding, stuffing and
  stamping (as before) .... 1.0 minute

Total time per statement .... 1.4 minutes

The new total time is:

1.4 minutes x 100 statements = 2.3 hours

ASHTON·TATE ■

The time required to complete this end-of-month task is thus reduced by about 77% (that is, 7.7 hours saved out of the original 10). For different offices with different billing volumes and equipment, the time saving can range from 50 to 80 percent. The true effect on your overall office efficiency is a lot better than that calculation indicates, however. The overhead is reduced, since you're not handling file folders and the computer doesn't lose its place every time the phone rings. Furthermore, part of that 2.3 hours is unattended machine time. Your staff can be doing other jobs while the statements are being processed.

ENHANCEMENTS

The time saving is certainly attractive, but it's not enough by itself to justify an investment in a computer. If you're only sending 100 statements, you're gaining 7.7 hours a month. Let's say your staff time (with overhead and benefits) costs you $12 an hour; then your saving is about $90 a month. If that's the only advantage, the computer will take on the order of five years to pay for itself![8] Usually we look for a payback period of three years or less for a good investment.

Our competition between the human and the computer hasn't been very fair so far. The only events we've judged are the ones the human is good at. That's like saying an automobile isn't worthwhile because it saves us only nine minutes in each trip to the corner store. The automobile wins hands down if we allow new events like hauling suitcases to the airport. Similarly, the computer can do things with very little extra effort on its part, which you wouldn't dream of asking your office staff to do manually (at least not without hiring another full-time employee).

MANAGEMENT REPORTS

Management Reports. You could ask your office manager to present you with a summary report of your receivables. One way for the manager to prepare it would be to copy the aging summary from the bottom of each statement onto a separate pad. (Insert that extra step into the proce-

ASHTON·TATE ■

dure outline, right after "Type a statement.") A typical report of this kind is shown in Figure 3.

That's a complete accounts receivable report. Yes, your office staff could prepare this report for you. The information was already retrieved from the files; it "only" had to be recopied onto another sheet of paper so you'd get a condensation that wouldn't require too much of your time to evaluate.

On second thought, even that is more information than you really want to see yourself. You're not going to fret over every balance that's 30 days old. The chore of reminding your clients has already been done by the statements that were just mailed out. All you want to see is a brief summary of the real problem cases—the ones who have owed you the same money for more than 90' days. That's called a delinquency report. It looks the same as the full receivables report, but it contains only clients who have a balance greater than $10.00 (or whatever minimum you want) in the Past-90 column. You'll probably want to call those clients personally or send them a special letter.

Hmmm.... If you're going to use the telephone for follow up, wouldn't it be nice if the report also contained the phone numbers? And also the date and amount of each client's last payment, in case there's a misunderstanding about whether they've paid. Or, if you're going to follow up by mail, someone has to type letters and envelopes.

It's ideas like these—these *wouldn't-it-be-nice-if's*—that are impractical to expect from a staff doing everything manually. To add phone numbers and last payment dates to the report, they'd have to copy additional information from the files while they're preparing the statements. (Insert yet another step into the outline.)

FINANCE CHARGES

Finance Charges. Another enhancement that is usually reserved for computerized offices is the addition of finance charges to overdue balances. A typical rate is 1.5% per month for everything more than 30 days past due. The primary reason for adding it isn't really the extra revenue it brings you. If, for example, you run a good-sized clinic with $40,000 in receivables a month, $10,000 of that might be overdue. The revenue from finance charges would be only $150 a month, just a fraction of one percent of your total receivables.

The real reason is to motivate your clients to pay promptly. You want to make them assign *some* priority to clearing that balance. Many people approach their personal debts in a very businesslike manner: they pay the most urgent ones first, then the ones carrying a finance charge, and finally the plain old bills to their friendly professionals. If the money supply runs out before they get to you, well . . . they did the best they could with what they had. Your objective is to raise your priority in their books.

Here's an outline of the steps to be added to the previous accounts receivable procedure:

Finance Charge Procedure

For each guarantor:

Add all the Past Dues to get a Balance Forward (as before).

Multiply that by 1.5% to get the Finance Charge.

Add the Finance Charge to Current (it's a new transaction).

(Continue with the old procedure from here on, with the adjusted current figure. Don't forget to show the new charge in the itemized list of this month's transactions.)

BUDGET PLANS

Budget Plans. Allowing your clients to pay in periodic installments is almost a mandatory service, if your charges for a single job or series of treatments tend to be large. For a manually-run office, however, budget plans open up several cracks for money to fall through. A very good filing system and monthly aging of your receivables are necessary. The aging method we described earlier is no longer adequate, because the amount due-and-payable is no longer the same as the *total* balance. The current amount due each month is now based on the agreed-upon monthly installment figure.

ASHTON·TATE ■

Guarantor's Name	Current	Past-30	Past-60	Past-90	Total
John Doe	100.00	50.00	150.00		300.00
Mary Smith	35.00				35.00
Percy Slow			75.00	95.00	170.00
.	.	.	.	.	.
.	.	.	.	.	.
.	.	.	.	.	.
.	.	.	.	.	.
TOTAL	5234.50	1875.00	524.70	125.00	7759.20

Figure 3. Computer-generated report showing total receivables

Since the total balance is no longer the simple sum of all the other columns (or the other drawers, to return to our desk analogy), we have to add a sixth drawer to hold the total. The content of the Total Drawer doesn't enter into the aging or finance charge calculations; it's there just to remind us when the payments are completed. Each new transaction (new service, payment, finance charge) is added to the total, of course.

If you're going to add this capability to your methods, you should go about it as methodically as you planned everything else. Discuss it with your staff. Then pull the looseleaf binder labelled "Procedures" down from the shelf. Turn to the Accounts Receivable procedure, and add the new steps to the outline. Here are the additions that make sense for our example, in the form of a new first step after aging but before typing the statement:

> For each guarantor:
>> Add the monthly installment figure to the current column. (The Current column will already contain a balance if there were any other new transactions during the month. Thus the installment is treated precisely the same as a new service; the service you rendered was a loaning of money.)
>> Add the past-due columns to get the Balance Forward as before.
>> Add the Balance Forward and Current to get the *Billable Total*.
>> If the Billable Total is greater than $1.00:
>>> Type a statement as before, but with one new figure added to the summary at the bottom: the true total balance. (It's a reminder of the client's total debt, even though it's not all due immediately.)

Don't forget that other office procedures will be affected as well. When you discuss the method of payment with your client, you need to have a firm policy on the amount of the first payment and the amount per month. Will you adjust the date of billing to accommodate your client? ("Mr. Doe, would you prefer to receive your statements on the 1st or the 15th?") And your methods for preparing your monthly management reports will change slightly.

As an extra touch, you might like to make up a book of coupons to make it easy for the client to remember the periodic payments. Each coupon should bear the expected amount and the date on which to mail it in. I've seen some dentists go so far as to include a supply of envelopes, stamped and addressed to the office. When the office staff receives the payment, they initial the coupon and mail it back as a receipt. The idea, of course, is to make it as easy as possible to make the payments on time.

Cycle Billing. Monthly billing is standard practice; your clients would likely be offended if they received a bill every two weeks. But that doesn't mean everyone has to be processed on the same day. Our examples have assumed end-of-month processing, but that has a few important disadvantages:

CYCLE BILLING

- •The end of the month becomes a dreaded chore, one that requires overtime work and lack of attention to the normal daily tasks.
- •Payments tend to be received in clumps, around the beginning of the second week of the month, which means another period of uneven work load and, more importantly, uneven cash flow.
- •Some clients might prefer a different billing date.

The obvious solution is to spread the billing over several days, but *how* to accomplish that isn't so obvious. Back to the planning stage! Get out the Procedures Manual and sharpen your pencils!

The easiest method in a manual office is to split up your accounts alphabetically. That's the method usually referred to as "cycle billing." Guarantors having a last name beginning with A through D are billed on the first Friday (or whatever) of the month. Those with E through L are done on the second Friday, and so on. Since your box of index cards is already organized in order of last

ASHTON·TATE ■

name, this method is fairly easy to implement. You simply
follow the same outline as before (aging and all) but stop
at the appropriate letter in your file. The only deficiency,
a minor one, is that you can't really accommodate individual preferences for billing date.

With a computerized data manager, it's possible to give
each client an individual billing date without relation to
name. The client file merely needs another item of information added. (In programmer's terms, the database needs
another field.) The computer can easily sift through the
file and process only those with the desired billing date;
the extra work means only a few more minutes (at most)
of unattended machine time. There's no danger that the
computer will absent-mindedly forget some of your
accounts; to a computer it makes just as much sense to
organize a file by a date as by a last name.

You should be careful, however, that the computer's
methods don't become too complex, especially when the
machine is first installed in your office. Keep it simple. I
recommend the straightforward cycle billing technique of
assigning a date by last name. (If an occasional client
really wants a different billing day, the computer should
allow its suggested date to be overridden.)

OPEN ITEM REPORT

The methods I've been describing so far are all part of
a relatively simple accounts receivable scheme. Think back
for a moment about the underlying principle: Transactions
are accumulated into drawers which are aged as a group,
one month at a time. Payments from the clients are simply
deducted from the oldest unpaid balance. There's no
provision for applying payment to a specific transaction. If
a client wants to pay you for one service you performed
and not another, our system won't handle it. All the
services are lumped together into drawers.

That limitation is acceptable, I think, for payments from
a client to a professional office. Reducing the oldest
balance is almost always good enough. If we were discussing large manufacturing companies or retail stores, where
purchase orders and partial shipments are common, then

we'd want to be able to treat some items as paid and others as still open. This "open item" method of handling receivables has disadvantages in complexity, however. When a payment comes in, you must somehow tell the data manager which item it should be applied to. Usually that means specifying some unique number that identifies each item—for example, a purchase order number or a claim number. That's extra work and extra data to be typed in and remembered. The complexity increases if the payment is partial, with some items being left "half-open." And to make sure that you haven't forgotten something that's still open from months ago, you need a new report called the open item report, which is a listing of all unpaid transactions.

There is one area, though, where open item tracking is useful in a professional office: insurance payments. An insurance company always itemizes which procedures a check applies to, and how much of the charged fee has been paid. The claim number serves as the identifier. Partial payments are not as great a complication as they might be in a retail store, since there's usually no need to chase down the remainder of the payment. Whatever the insurance doesn't cover will be receivable from the client; it can simply be lumped into the drawers as we've been doing so far.

In this case, the extra work of keeping track of claim numbers and open items is worth it. If a claim you've submitted is unduly delayed or even forgotten, you want to know exactly which one it is and which procedures were on it. That's the information you need when you complain to the company.

If that's the only justification for open-item tracking, however, there may be a better way to keep an eye on the insurance companies than complicating the accounts receivable. In the next chapter on physicians we'll see a separate method for tracking claims, by which errors other than just slow payments can be caught.

ASHTON·TATE ■

Yet another capability you should expect from your data manager is a recap of all the day's transactions, including services actually performed as well as payments received for past services. This daily journal can be thought of as another management report, but it doesn't try to analyze or categorize the transactions; it's just an exhaustive list. You might frequently decide not to read it at all. But it should still be printed and saved, or at least should be printable when you feel like it, for the following reasons:

Backup. It serves as a paper copy of the day's transactions, a comforting hands-on record in case all else goes wrong. (We'll talk in the last chapter about ways to make sure all else *doesn't* go wrong, but just in case....)

Cash Receipt. The daily journal should include a total of all the hard cash and checks received during the day. All it requires is a simple running total, and it gives you a double-check against the contents of the cash drawer. Some computerized systems will go a step further and print a deposit slip, in case your volume is large enough to warrant daily trips to the night deposit box.

Security. A long-standing principle of financial control is to separate the handling of money from the accounting for it. Otherwise the temptation for sloppiness and "borrowing" is just too great. "Oh my! I left my lunch money at home today. I'll just borrow two dollars from the cash drawer till tomorrow." The opportunity should never be allowed to arise. In large companies that means cash is disbursed by a department completely removed from the one that authorizes it. In your office you're unlikely to go that far, but the existence of a daily summary that can be perused by a second person (whether it is or not) is enough to remove the problem.

In some computerized systems (especially older ones) the daily journal is a mandatory report. These systems save the day's transactions in a temporary file, and don't actually add them to the books until you've had a chance

DAILY JOURNAL

ASHTON·TATE ■

to check the entries for errors. They are then added ("posted") in one large batch. In systems like this, the daily journal is actually the listing you use for your error-checking.

Better Understanding. Automated aging and management reports give you a much better sense of the health of your business than you're likely to get with a manual system. You can judge whether your overall receivables picture is improving or getting worse, by comparing various indicators to what they were last month and last year. Typical indicators are:

- •Total past-due amount as a percentage of total receivables. (Are your collection efforts weakening? Perhaps you just lost a valuable office manager. Maybe some other change in your professional practice is rubbing your clients the wrong way.)
- •Past-90 amount as a percentage of total receivables. (A rise here is a real sign of danger. Look back through the previous months to see where the increase began, and ask yourself what happened then.)
- •Total receivables as a percentage of total income. (It isn't necessarily bad to see your receivables on the rise. It may indicate a shift in clientele, or a general economic downturn in your area.)
- •Budget payments as a percentage of your total receivables. (Another benign indicator. Budget plan activity might be up merely because your average bill has increased. Are you taking on fewer but more lucrative cases?)

You should pick your own indicators according to what makes sense in your business. The important thing is to have some consistent and objective guideline. And it should almost always be a ratio or a percentage rather than just a total dollar figure. It's quite possible to

BENEFITS FROM ACCOUNTS RECEIVABLE MANAGEMENT

ASHTON·TATE ■

increase your *total* income, for example, while taking a beating on real profit. An upturn in your *total* receivables might be good or bad, depending on whether your income is increasing as well, and depending on how badly you need cash now.

After a year or so of this kind of analysis, you'll be able to predict your future cash flow with accuracy. You'll have an idea of seasonal variations. You'll develop a rule of thumb for how much of your receivables usually end up as uncollectable. Professional accountants in large companies can often predict the uncollectable amount very closely; they call it the Allowance for Doubtful Accounts. One typical rule of thumb is three percent of the total receivables. Another is five percent of the current amount, plus 25 percent of the Past-30, plus 50 percent of the Past-60, plus 75 percent of the Past-90.

Using your Accounts Receivable as an Asset. Technically, to an accountant, receivables are an asset just as your cash and your equipment are assets. That asset can be used to bring in immediate cash if you need it. The most common method is to get a short-term loan from a bank with your receivables as collateral. Some people mistakenly view this practice as a last-ditch attempt by a floundering business. The fact is that you're unlikely to get such a loan unless your business is healthy. Frequently the reason for the loan is an expansion into a new or larger office.

A second method, less common for professional offices, is called factoring. This is essentially the selling of your receivables to a bank or other financial institution. You're paid the book value, less an allowance for uncollectables, and less a discount which constitutes the buyer's profit. After the sale your clients might be asked to make their future payments to the institution.

In either case the lending institution will want to analyze your past and present income. Here's where a computerized system is invaluable. You'll be able to arm yourself with daily transaction summaries; monthly and quarterly reports of receivables, complete with aging; and your own estimate of the uncollectable percentage.

ASHTON·TATE ■

Computer-generated reports always look more authentic than hand-typed ones. However, the difference is more than just looks, because the bank knows that the computer is recording every adjustment and error, and can reproduce the report from the original data with ease if it is felt to be necessary.

Faster Attention to Delinquent Accounts. The best way to handle slow paying clients is to contact them as soon as the problem becomes apparent; that is, as soon as it passes your definition of seriously overdue (usually 60 or 90 days). Fast action is possible with either a manual or a computerized data manager, but the computer makes the work easier. If you prefer to send a letter as your means of contact, the computer can automatically generate personalized form letters including the balance due and the length of time since the last payment. Or you might prefer phone contact, making use of the delinquency report we discussed earlier—a list of names, phone numbers, and payment history. If the problem occurs with a client who is still seeing you regularly, make sure you have a report of the account history in your hands for the next appointment.

Secure Audit Trail. A computer will not eliminate errors by you and your staff. In either a manual or an automated office, charges and payments will occasionally be entered incorrectly. In a manual office, however, the most expedient solution to the error is to change it—erase it and reenter it—without bothering to make a note that the error occurred. That opens the possibility for sloppiness, or even minor theft from the cash drawer, and it's rarely obvious after the fact what caused the mistake.

A computer system, if it's well designed, will not allow errors to be corrected without recording the reason and the amount. Often, the system will not allow the error to be merely changed; a new entry will have to be made as an adjustment or reversal. The adjustment is made just as if it were a new transaction, and it subsequently appears on all the end-of-month summaries. Indeed, such adjustments are in fact emphasized in the reports by placing

ASHTON·TATE ■

them in a column by themselves. There is much less chance of an error being misinterpreted, and virtually no chance of petty pilferage going unnoticed. Usually the mistakes are honest, and seeing them in a report may tell you where your staff is being overworked or misinformed.

OTHER ACCOUNTING FUNCTIONS: PROFITABILITY ANALYSIS

If you were to collect together all the daily journal reports for a month, you would have a very long itemized listing of every service you had performed. To make more sense out of it, you could arrange all the services into logical groups, then add your income within each group. From that you'd get a good idea of what facets of your business are bringing in the most money. That's the idea behind a profitability report. If you're a dentist, for example, you might like to know that although 22 percent of your procedures were diagnostic in nature, only six percent of your income came from that group. You might also like to know that one of the professionals in the office (you, of course) is bringing in 60 percent of the revenues. A simple report for a one-dentist office might look like Figure 4.

To be accurate, what I've just described is more properly called a productivity analysis. It only shows you your production, not your profit, since it doesn't take into account the cost of each item. In a professional office, the cost of each item usually means *time*. Your time is the raw material from which the services are created. If you were to keep track of the minutes you spent on each service during the month—to the closest 15 minutes is accurate enough—you'd be able to add to the above report more informative numbers, like dollars per hour. Perhaps prosthodontics isn't your most profitable group, as suggested by the report. Maybe each crown or inlay takes you five times as long as other procedures.

That's enough for now to give you the idea. The full-blown profitability analysis will be developed in more detail in the lawyers' chapter, since that's the profession that places the greatest emphasis on billing on a time basis.

The calculation of payroll is a function that doesn't really lie within the scope of this book. For the typical professional office we're concerned with here, payroll is a number-crunching job, not data management. There are few decisions to be made; all your employees probably live and work in the same state, so the calculation is the same for all of them. And the task is easy enough to carry out manually (for a typical office with fewer than ten employees) so that a computer doesn't offer much of a time saving.

I'm mentioning payroll briefly because it's a function often included in the realm of "computerized accounting," and you're likely to hear about it. It is useful if you decide to go "all the way" and automate all your books, with a general ledger and financial statements. In that case the computer will have to know what your payroll expenses are anyway, in order to keep track of your total picture. You could continue to write your checks manually and enter the figures into the computer, but you might as well let the computer do the whole job. That way you'll even get your paychecks printed for you.

The idea behind the management of accounts payable is to get the greatest mileage out of your cash on hand. Pay your most important bills first—the ones due now or the ones that give you a discount if you pay now.

This is another function that, in my opinion, isn't a big benefit to the average professional. You don't make large purchases of raw materials from many different vendors. The total amount you owe to your suppliers isn't as perilously close to your total income as it would be if you were a factory or a supermarket.

The proper management of payables is nevertheless a good example of data management. We can see that by looking at the steps involved: prioritization and decision-making. As usual, I'll put the steps into an outline:

Procedure for Accounts Payable Management
List all your outstanding bills.
Put the list in order of priority:

Service Group	No. done this Month	% of Total No.	Total $ this Month	% of Total $
Diagnostic	210	22	2,520.00	6
Preventive	340	36	6,120.00	14
Restorative	190	20	5,320.00	12
Endodontics	84	9	13,440.00	30
Periodontics	31	3	2.480.00	6
Prosthodontics	65	7	13,650.00	30
Others	32	3	1,280.00	3

Figure 4. Profitability analysis

overdue bills,

those about to become overdue,

those that allow a discount if paid now,

all the rest.

Decide how far down the list you want to pay, by rules such as:

Pay as many as you can (distribute all your cash).

Pay out as much cash as you feel like releasing.

Pay just the important ones and leave "all the rest" till next month.

Print the checks.

Enter the amounts paid in your books. (Decrease the payables, of course, and also enter the disbursements in your cash journal if you're keeping a general ledger.)

INVENTORY CONTROL

The ability to keep a close eye on inventory, to know what's on hand and how long it's been there, is particularly valuable to pharmacists. This application will be featured in the chapter devoted to them (Chapter 7).

Doctors and dentists are less likely to care about the dollar value of the items on hand, and the size of their inventory is usually small enough to handle manually. They do need to exercise control on sensitive items like narcotics, drugs with a limited shelf life, and samples under analysis. Those of you in large clinics or hospitals, who have a large enough stock of such items to make computerized inventory control a consideration, can refer to the discussion in Chapter 7.

GENERAL LEDGER

A general ledger system is designed to give you a complete financial picture of your business. It's a central collection point for all the other accounting entries: cash income and outgo, receivables, payables, inventory, and payroll. The general ledger is the only application that isn't designed to deal with individual transactions, bills, or clients. It *summarizes* all of those, purely for your management information.

ASHTON·TATE ■

In order to present a total financial picture, the general ledger has to know about every transaction that affects your assets or liabilities, which is the same as saying *every* transaction. For example, you'd need to tell the computer the amount involved and the reason for all of the following: rent, paychecks to your staff, money withdrawn by yourself (whether by regular paycheck or not), equipment purchases, loans, and adjustments to inventory.

If you're automated to the extent that the computer already knows all those things—it prints your paychecks, tracks your payables, monitors your inventory, and balances your checkbook—then a general ledger is a logical addition to the system. It will give you extra information with little or no extra work. This situation will usually apply only to the larger businesses: clinics, hospitals, large law firms, and chains of stores. On the other hand, if you're not that automated you'll have to enter all those transactions manually. That doesn't mean you can't have a general ledger, just that it will require a little extra human time at the keyboard. If your inventory and payroll are small enough not to warrant computerization to start with, then the extra work shouldn't be too difficult.

The real determinant of whether your business should have a general ledger, then, is your own management style. If you want to know what your net worth is, then do it. If, like many independent professionals, you'd just as soon not have your complete picture collected onto any one piece of paper, you certainly don't need a general ledger!

At the end of any given period of time, usually quarterly or yearly, you'll be able to get these two summary reports:

> •A financial statement (also called a balance sheet), which shows your total assets and liabilities, and your business's net worth (whatever's left over). Thus, the financial statement presents a snapshot of your current status. If there are clearly defined departments within your business, you should be

able to see similar statements for each of
them.

• An income statement, which shows the
in-and-out flows which led to the current
status. All the income and expense categories
will be summarized to give you a better
picture of how your net profit got to be what
it is for the period.

Along with either report, you should be able to get a
comparison to the previous month, quarter, or year. This
is a mandatory capability, since a number all by itself (net
profit is ten percent of income) is hard to interpret unless
you can tell that it's rising or falling, very much like a
barometer reading.

Client list management is the manipulation of your
homegrown database—generated from a little personal data
about your clients, plus your accumulated daily transactions. You may have seen computerized spreadsheets,
which manipulate numbers and answer questions like
"what if?". Client list management is concerned more with
text than numbers, with comparing and filtering more
than statistics. The typical question is "Who?" or "Show
me."

The value to you as a professional is that all your past
paperwork becomes an *asset* rather than a headache. For
little or no extra effort, you gain improved understanding
of your business and better-focussed, more timely communications with your clients. But notice that the benefits are
not the kind providing tangible cost savings. Improved
understanding, better contact, or any of the specific examples in the chapter—it's hard to say any of them save you
money. (This can be contrasted with the more quantifiable
benefits in the next chapters, such as accounts receivable.)
The payoff from client list management comes, sooner or
later, from an increased *volume* of business: more loyal
clients, more frequent visits in response to your reminders.

The major lessons to remember are:

**SUMMARY:
CLIENT LIST
MANAGEMENT**

ASHTON·TATE ■

•Plan ahead. Make up the kinds of questions that are important to you before you design your database. Decide which pieces of information you'll need in order to answer your questions. Then include those fields into your database.

•Don't try for perfection at the outset. You can always regroup later.

•If you're unsure whether or not a particular field will have value later on, include it. That's a corollary of the last point. You can always get rid of excess data; you can't add it if it wasn't saved.

•To reap the full benefit of your homegrown database, you need to understand the fundamental concepts of data retrieval: how your inquiries are answered; how to combine several conditions with "and's" and "or's" to define exactly what you want, when you're asking for something that's just plain hard for your system to answer; and when to settle for an easier question. You don't have to be a programmer, but neither should you allow yourself to be spoon-fed, to be confined to whatever reports the system designer allowed for. Nobody knows better than yourself what questions to ask in your profession.

In considering the common accounting functions, don't forget the reasons behind them: to control and understand your business *objectively*; to let you analyze your business as an entity separate from your profession. All of the applications we've discussed can be performed well by a small computer in your office, but not all of them are of great benefit to the average professional.

ACCOUNTS RECEIVABLE AND OTHER ACCOUNTING FUNCTIONS

Accounts receivable finds a place in any office that allows delayed payments, whether by extending credit to the clients or by billing insurance carriers or other third-party agencies. The data manager's goal is to remember

all outstanding balances and their age, and to issue
prompt and informative statements to the clients. There
are several possible enhancements to this basic idea:

- •Management reports make it easy for you to
picture the status of your overall receivables.
The mandatory ones are a full report of all
balances with aging, and a delinquents-only
report.
- •Three variations in the billing process are
budget plans (allowing balances to be paid in
regular installments), cycle billing (spreading
your statements over the month), and finance
charges (adding a penalty for overdue
accounts). Each of them represents an extra
workload for human data managers, but
they're taken in stride by a good computerized system.
- •An open item report facilitates the tracking
of unpaid transactions, which is especially
helpful if insurance or other third-party coverage is involved.

An important characteristic of receivables management is
a secure audit trail. It should not be possible to modify
past transactions without leaving an adjusting entry as a
trail. Usually there's a grace period of a day during which
corrections can be easily made; if so, a daily journal is
listed to aid in your error checking.

A profitability analysis is also a management report, but
it includes cash payments as well as receivables. It classifies your transactions according to segments of your
business, to clarify which segments are the most
profitable. An analysis of dollars per hour is an optional
extra feature of this report.

Other applications are a general ledger, inventory,
payroll, and accounts payable. Of these, the general
ledger, which presents a unified summary of your income
and net worth, is the only one beneficial to a wide range
of offices. It rounds out the picture for the more busi-
ness-minded of you who want to understand your practice

ASHTON·TATE ■

well—as well as you would a separate company asking for investment (which in some ways your business is).

Notes

1. The morale-building effect of involving the workers is often called the "Hawthorne effect." The name comes from an early experiment in an industrial plant in which two groups of workers, one working in an improved environment and the other staying in the old one, were *both* observed to become more productive. The conclusion? That it was the attention to the workers' ideas and concerns, not the change in environment, that motivated them.

2. The program is written in a data management language called dBASE II[R], published by Ashton-Tate, Culver City, Calif. Several similar languages exist for microcomputers and minicomputers that will perform the same task with roughly the same program structure.

3. If, for instance, your client Mrs. Smith calls with a misunderstanding about her last bill, you can review her balance and date of last payment in a few seconds, and be sure that your information is up to date. With modern programming techniques and hardware, that recall can be accomplished in only a few seconds, even with thousands of records. This is a capability often emphasized in computer demonstrations. But if the computer is already busy doing something else (like printing statements), and it's designed to do only one thing at a time (as most of them still are), then you can't use it for instant recall. Hence, unless you want to tell Mrs. Smith to wait for you to call back, you'll have to pull out your paper records anyway.

   It is possible to add a second station (screen and keyboard) to some systems to get around this, but this multi-user feature can add at least a couple of thousand dollars to the price of the system. A better solution is now available on a few of the newest microcomputers, called "concurrency." It allows you, with just the minimum single station, to retrieve your data while the statement processing continues merrily along.

4. I find an interesting parallel here between small business and big industry. American industry has been faulted for taking too short-term a view of profits, and not doing enough research and investment for the long term. If you use your computer only as a fancy filing cabinet and fast typewriter, you're falling into the same trap. The great advantage you have is that this long-term research doesn't require any additional capital investment, and very little extra time.

5. Some computer-related books give you illustrations far removed from what will actually work on a computer. Their intention is good (they're trying to avoid blinding you with the trees of syntax before you've seen the forest of the concepts), but they tend to make your first experience with a computer somewhat frustrating. Rest assured that, although I'm trying to illustrate a "universal recipe" for inquiries, the recipe *is* followed closely by database management languages. For example, dBASE II uses the form:

   DISPLAY ALL (fields) for (condition)
   where you fill in the specific fields and condition. For our first example:

   DISPLAY ALL name,date for service="WILL".and.state="NY"
   There are a few computerese details you have to get used to—such as the quotation marks around the data and the periods around the "and"—but the similarity to our "Show me" examples is clear. Since you're allowed to name the fields in your database any way *you* like, the inquiry retains a strong resemblance to English.

ASHTON·TATE ■

6. The illustration I'm about to give is real, although the exact words and punctuation might vary from one system to another. The illustration is based on my own experience with a particular data management program (dBASE II) and a particular word processing program (Spellbinder®). The key features to look for in other systems are: the data management language's ability to save the result of an inquiry in an intermediate file (often called "print-to-disk"), and the word processor's ability to merge that saved list into a document (such as MailMerge® in WordStar™).

7. I use the term "guarantors" to mean the person financially responsible for paying the bill, usually the head of the household. Many of you may simply refer to that person or agency as the "account." I prefer to avoid confusion with the more technical meaning of that word, as in "accounts receivable."

8. When I talk about the computer "paying for itself," I'm thinking in terms of a very simple straight-line reckoning. The last chapter will cover other methods of analyzing the cost of a system, but this is good enough for now. If the cost of a computer system is $10,000, the true cost to you after tax credits and depreciation is very roughly $5,000. Dividing by the saving per month (ignoring inflation) gives $5,000 divided by $90, or a payback period of 55 months.

ASHTON·TATE ■

Chapter Four

Physicians

Now that we've looked at the data management functions shared by many professionals, it's time to get more specific. We'll look first at physicians. If you are one, you know you have a few problems unlikely to be found in any other profession. We'll begin with a brief analysis of the common applications discussed in Chapter 3 to show where a physician's office needs a few extra features. Then we'll see some entirely new problems.

Remember that all of these functions are related to the business side of your practice. There is another whole world of applications for small computers on the technical side that we won't even touch: medical research, the automated analysis of tests and samples, and the computer-assisted diagnosis and interpretation of results.

The logic behind accounts receivable has been covered in Chapter 3, so there's no need to explain it again. There is one additional concern, however, that I seem to hear most often from physicians: a concern for maintaining a relationship of trust with their patients. Even though doctors understand the need for management of their accounts, they will not often resort to finance charges and collection agencies.

ACCOUNTS RECEIVABLE

ASHTON·TATE ■

That doesn't mean they don't want to *know* who's behind in payments. I admire the approach taken by Dr. Chris Reilly, a gynecologist in Paterson, NJ.[1] He uses a computer to keep track of his receivables, but steps in personally whenever there's a billing problem with a patient. He refuses to use a collection agency because he feels "there's a distinct relationship between unpaid bills and dissatisfied patients." If the reason for the slow payment is unhappiness with the service that was performed, then a collection notice might goad the patient into legal action. Instead, he sends a questionnaire to let the person express any dissatisfaction, and to give himself a chance to repair the relationship. The questionnaire is automatically printed by the computer, of course, so that it's personalized with the patient's name, amount due, and services rendered.

PROFITABILITY ANALYSIS

The same Dr. Reilly provides a good example in the use of profitability analysis as a decision-making aid. He was notified that the malpractice insurance rates would be lowered for gynecologists who did not do any obstetrics, and had to decide whether a particular procedure was profitable enough to warrant the extra cost of insurance. The difference in premium amounted to $1400 a year. The profitability analysis, however, showed him in minutes that he'd earned $20,000 from assisting in caesarean deliveries alone, making it worthwhile to pay the extra premium.

In that example it was sufficient to know the dollars earned per procedure. But as we pointed out before, the ability to view profitability on a time basis is sometimes desirable. The practitioners most likely to need this are the ones whose services don't fall into clearly discrete procedures, the ones whose fees are at least partially based on an hourly rate. That includes physical therapists, chiropractors, psychologists, and psychiatrists.

FORM HANDLING

We've seen a few examples already of what I call form handling, which is simply the use of a computer as an

ASHTON·TATE ■

automatic typewriter. It's not a very exciting capability, but it can save many hours of human time. Computers excel at rearranging information from their memories into some new order before putting it on paper. The printing of statements in Chapter Three was a good example; we showed that a time saving of from 50 to 80 percent is reasonable. The personalized letters in our discussion of client list management represented another kind of form handling. Neither of those chores was impossible to do by hand—the computer was simply faster.

There are new functions in the area of form handling that only a computer can carry out, including the elimination of forms altogether! Automated offices are becoming common enough that third parties are beginning to accept data entry directly from your computer. This makes perfectly good sense. Why should you make your computer print out a complicated form (when printing is the slowest operation) just so it can be mailed (with the additional risk of loss) to someone who's going to enter the data back into a computer (the most error-prone step in the system)?

Clearly, it is more effective to trade data directly between computers (in "machine-readable form"), but this capability is slow in coming. There are problems to be worked out in standardization. It would be better for everyone involved if all the third parties accepted the data in the same standard format; otherwise your office computer might need a separate program to prepare the data for each company.

The companies may require standardization on your end as well. They may dictate which computers are acceptable in your office if you expect to talk to theirs. They may require an initial test or probationary period to make sure your system doesn't cause more than its normal share of errors, before you can become a full partner.

There are also problems to be worked out in the area of security. Before the insurance companies will let hundreds of small office computers talk to theirs, they want to be *sure* that nobody can abuse the privilege by

ASHTON·TATE ■

getting into the company's files or into some other practitioner's files. That has always been a concern, of course, but it's something else again to publish a phone number and invite outsiders to look!

Basically, only two ways are used at present to exchange data in machine-readable form. In the first method, your office mails to the insurance company a magnetic disk containing your data. Virtually all business computers are able to store information on these flexible magnetic disks, popularly called floppies. This method still relies on the transfer of a physical object, but the object is *much* smaller than the corresponding paperwork would be. One little $5 floppy disk can hold as much information as several hundred claim forms. More importantly, there's no need for a human to retype (re-enter) all the information.

The "floppy-in-the-mail" approach has been taken by Medicaid in New York State. Because all computers do not necessarily put data on the disks in the same way, McAuto, the company that handles all the Medicaid claims, will only accept a floppy disk in one of several popular formats: Apple, Vector Graphic, or IBM. A further aspect in standardization is the size and order of the individual pieces of data. The insurance company has to know that the first item on the disk will always have the same meaning—let's say a patient number—and the next item (12 characters later) will be a claim number, and so on. McAuto publishes a detailed listing of the organization it expects. You can see the standardization problem in action here.

The second method, called Electronic Claims Submission (ECS), uses the telephone. Data can be transferred as mere beeps and whistles over the existing phone lines, untouched by human hands! Although the technology behind this capability can be fairly complicated, the concept is easy to understand. Pretend you want to send a very important claim to the insurance company for immediate service. Luckily, you have an inside contact at the company, your niece, the same inexperienced person you had to train in Chapter 3. You call her and, to make sure there are no errors, proceed to read the claim information to her one character at a time, in the same order as it appears on the claim form. "The patient's name is S-M-I-T-H-comma-J-O-H-N. The address is 1-2-4-space-M-A-I-N-space-S-T-R-E-E-T."

That's essentially what happens in Electronic Claims Submission. One character at a time, in a predefined order, is converted to sounds and sent by phone. Fortunately the speed is a lot faster than in our parable. The most common transmission rates for small computers are 30 or 120 characters per second. So, if a typical claim involves 1000 characters (letters, numbers, spaces), the whole thing will take either eight seconds or 33 seconds respectively.

I've simplified the process, of course. There also must be some way to know when an error has occurred. For example, you might have asked your niece to read all the information back to you at the end; that's one form of error-checking.

Blue Shield of Northern California is an insurance carrier that now offers this capability. One cardiologist in that area, who had already experienced a one-month improvement in his cash flow by installing a computer, found that he chopped another two weeks off the payment delay with ECS.[2] The direct submission bypassed the lag time inherent in the mail, entry, and validation steps.

ECS is clearly the wave of the future. When it is available, the next logical speed-up can occur: electronic claims *inquiry*. This is also offered by Blue Shield of Northern California. The doctor can ask the company's computer to display a summary of all claims pending, paid, or held up.

Soon, the only paper changing hands may be the final payment check, and even that isn't really necessary. Banks have been talking about electronic funds transfer for some time, but the idea hasn't really caught on with the public—possibly because the individual never seems to have any control of the process. Perhaps that will change if you're able to see the exact amount of the check as it

ASHTON·TATE ■

leaves the insurance company, and later verify that it really has been received by the bank.

THIRD-PARTY
TRACKING

A characteristic shared by all third-party payment plans is the lack of face-to-face contact. Impersonal forms are mailed in one direction, and checks are mailed in the other (usually accompanied by even more forms). Patients are invariably identified by account numbers and group numbers. Your services are identified by procedure codes. There's a whole mess of data to be managed here!

Third parties are probably the greatest single reason for the installation of a computerized data manager. As I lamented in the pessimistic part of Chapter 1, you need your own computer just to defend yourself against all the bureaucracies. Their computers manipulate the numbers and codes generated by your practice in ways that are seldom decipherable and sometimes wrong,[3] and regurgitate a check that has a very tangible impact on your wallet. The situation has a lot in common with the "taxation without representation" dispute back in 1776. One way to protect yourself (like the Bostonians who threw the tea in the harbor and did without) is simply to refuse to deal with third parties. Many practitioners have made that decision and only accept payments directly from their patients. If the patients can recoup some of the fee by submitting claims on their own, that's fine—but it's their problem.

A better defense, and a more profitable one, is to stand up to the agencies. Catch their mistakes and slow payments, and refuse to accept them. How to deal with the agencies as an equal will be clear after the next few sections.

WHAT'S THE
PROBLEM?

First, you have to be aware that the problem exists! Some of you, even though you're physicians dealing with third parties daily, may not be fully aware of what can happen. In a nutshell, you're losing money if you trust the third parties not to make mistakes.

For a specific example, let's step through the normal process of submitting a Medicare claim in New York State. Although the details of this process may vary in your area, the conclusion will still be valid. (Even though Medicare is a federally regulated program, the different companies administering it in each area are allowed some leeway in interpretation of the rules.)

Assume that a hypothetical patient named Janice Reeve is being treated by you for a broken hip—a fracture at the upper end of the femur to be more precise. (I'll describe this case in detail for the benefit of non-physicians.)

Step 1: The Treatment. You determine that the fracture is serious enough to require an incision to repair the fracture before applying a cast. The technical description of the procedure is an "open reduction." In other cases an incision might not have been required; then it would be a closed reduction. If an internal metal pin is needed for support, that's known as internal fixation. Further classifications are possible to describe whether the wound is open or closed, and to include other types of fractures and methods of repair. A complete description might get as complicated as "open reduction of closed intertrochanteric fracture of the femur with internal fixation."

Don't forget that the number of possibilities is further multiplied by the number of bones in the body. Even then we've only covered one branch of medicine, the one concerned with the musculo-skeletal system. Faced with this bewildering number of possible descriptions for procedures, the American Medical Association formulated a set of standard codes called CPT codes (Current Procedural Terminology). As the AMA explains, "The purpose of the terminology is to provide a uniform language that will accurately designate medical, surgical and diagnostic services, and will thereby provide an effective means for reliable, nationwide communication among physicians, patients, and third parties."[4] A sample of the kind of codes you'll see in the standard listing is shown in Figure 1.

In this case, the open reduction of a femoral fracture corresponds to CPT code 27244. That's the number you'll probably use internally in your own office, and the one you might use if you prepare a claim to any of several insurance companies.

Step 2: Claim Submission. Unfortunately, this particular claim is going to Medicare. Medicare in New York doesn't use the CPT standard! It has its own own set of Medicare codes. A sample from their book is shown in Figure 2. The code to be used in the claim, therefore, is 0874. That's entered in the last half of the claim form. (For simplicity we're ignoring the X-ray and any other procedures that might have been performed.) A Medicare claim form is shown in Figure 3.

As the preparer of this form, you may refuse to look up and use the Medicare codes and instead enter a description of the procedure in words. That's equivalent to asking the Medicare agency to perform the code look-up for you, which of course creates an opportunity for errors to creep in. In our sample form we've entered both the code and the description, but they're not both necessary.

You'll notice from the claim form that there are other "complications." The "Place" column asks for another code, this time a letter, to designate where the service was performed; the "O" specifies the physician's Office. The "Type" code is a single digit which Medicare uses to refer to the general class of procedure; the "1" means surgery. Finally, the "Diagnosis Code" is a number specifying the cause of the condition or disease. It comes from yet another standard listing (in three volumes!) called the ICD-9-CM codes, an International Classification of Diseases.

The "Accept Assignment" field is a very important one for our discussion. If you check "Yes" you're agreeing to accept Medicare's idea of the standard fee for the procedure. Their standard fees are derived from a complicated, not well publicized formula, based on the procedure; your "profile" of fees charged for similar procedures in the past; and the profile of other doctors in your area. If

ASHTON·TATE ■

27230 Treatment of closed femoral fracture, proximal end, neck; without manipulation

27232   with manipulation including skeletal traction

27234 Treatment of open femoral fracture, proximal end, neck, with uncomplicated soft tissue closure, with manipulation (including skeletal traction)

27235 Treatment of closed or open femoral fracture, proximal end, neck, in situ pinning of undisplaced or impacted fracture

27236 Open treatment of closed or open femoral fracture, proximal end, neck, internal fixation or prosthetic replacement

27238 Treatment of closed intertrochanteric or pertrochanteric femoral fracture; without manipulation

27240   with manipulation (including skeletal traction)

27242 Treatment of open intertrochanteric or pertrochanteric femoral fracture, with uncomplicated soft tissue closure (including traction)

27244 Open treatment of closed or open intertrochanteric or pertrochanteric femoral fracture, with internal fixation

27246 Treatment of closed greater trochanteric fracture, without manipulation

27248 Open treatment of closed or open greater trochanteric fracture, with or without internal or external skeletal fixation

Figure 1. Sample listing from CPT codes

LOWER EXTREMITIES

FEMUR, NECK OF FEMUR

1	0865	SIMPLE, CLOSED REDUCTION			56	3
		1461.75	1428.40	1754.10		
		877.10	1461.75	1754.10		

1	0866	COMPOUND, CLOSED REDUCTION			56	4
		1358.40	1206.60	1024.40		
		772.80	888.60	870.00		

1	0867	SIMPLE OR COMPOUND, OPEN REDUCTION WITH OR WITHOUT PROSTHETIC REPLACEMENT OF THE HEAD			56	6
		2533.70	1887.20	1461.75		
		1413.00	1949.00	1461.75		

INTERTROCHANTERIC

1	0872	SIMPLE, CLOSED REDUCTION			56	3
		1461.75	1559.20	1656.70		
		779.60	1559.20	1559.20		

1	0873	COMPOUND, CLOSED REDUCTION			56	4
		1358.40	1206.60	1024.40		
		772.80	888.60	870.00		

1	0874	SIMPLE OR COMPOUND, OPEN REDUCTION			56	6
		2533.70	1949.00	1461.75		
		1413.00	1949.00	1247.40		

SLIPPED EPIPHYSIS

1	0877	CLOSED REDUCTION			56	3
		1018.80	905.00	768.30		
		579.60	666.50	652.50		

Figure 2. Sample listing from Medicare codes

your fee is greater than what Medicare considers normal and customary, you accept the lower amount. Another consequence of accepting Assignment is that the subsequent payment and other correspondence is sent to you, not to the patient.

Step 3: Payment and Explanation of Benefits. The calculation of your payment is the first step that really uses numbers as "numbers." Assuming you've accepted Assignment, Medicare approves an amount for each procedure as we just discussed. (Incidentally, the amount may be zero if the procedure is a repetition, a second treatment within a certain time interval since the first treatment, or one that the agency feels should have been included in a prior treatment.)

Of that approved amount, Medicare pays 80 percent and the patient is expected to pay the other 20 percent. There is, however, a deductible to be satisfied—the patient is expected to pay the first $75 of charges each year. So the full calculation is:

Medicare Payment Calculation

(Amount approved by Medicare) - (Remaining deductible)
= Balance Payable
(Balance Payable) x 80 percent = Amount Paid by Medicare
(Balance Payable) x 20 percent + (Deductible)
= Amount Billed to Patient

The remaining 20 percent, plus the deductible, if any, is billed to the patient. To clarify this, let's say the patient's deductible was already satisfied this year. If Medicare believes the customary fee for the surgery is $600, a little less than what you charged, then:

$$
\begin{aligned}
\text{(Amount approved)} - \text{(Deductible)} &= \text{Balance Payable} \\
\$600.00 - 0 &= 600.00 \\
\text{(Balance Payable)} \times 80 \text{ percent} &= \text{Amount Paid} \\
600.00 \times 80 \text{ percent} &= 480.00 \\
\text{(Balance Payable)} \times 20 \text{ percent} &= \text{Amount Billed} \\
600.00 \times 20 \text{ percent} &= 120.00
\end{aligned}
$$

Medicare attempts to explain all this on a form called the Explanation of Benefits it sends along with the check. (See Figure 4.)

Several claims will typically be included in the same Explanation of Benefits and the check. Here we've shown only one. The form is difficult enough to read as it is. With the HIC number (identifying the patient) and the IC number (identifying the particular claim), this form probably holds the record for the longest sequence of digits (73 of them) generated from one simple procedure.

Step 4: Patient Billing. Finally (and this is typically a few months after the procedure was performed), you're ready to bill the patient for his/her 20 percent. Back in Chapter Three we discussed billing and other aspects of accounts receivable management, so there's no need to cover it in detail again. If you've been using a computerized system to process all the claims so far, then your work is essentially over at this point. The system will know that there's still an amount that's receivable.

There are just two more points to make about billing before we're done with this example. First, you may be tempted to forgive—and forget—the amounts due from your patients. Don't do it! If you routinely forget about the remainders not covered by Medicare, the administrator is likely to argue that your real fees are the amounts you're settling for, not the higher ones you're putting on the claim forms. Your customary fee profile will then be revised downward to match what you appear to be charging, with the result that you'll get 80 percent of what you're getting now. You must print, mail, and diligently track those bills.

HEALTH INSURANCE
CLAIM FORM
READ INSTRUCTIONS BEFORE COMPLETING OR SIGNING THIS FORM

TYPE OR PRINT ☐ MEDICARE ☐ MEDICAID ☐ OTHER

PATIENT & INSURED (SUBSCRIBER) INFORMATION

1 PATIENT'S NAME (First name middle initial last name)	2 PATIENT'S DATE OF BIRTH	3 INSURED'S NAME (First name middle initial last name)

4 PATIENT'S ADDRESS (Street city state ZIP code)	5 PATIENT'S SEX MALE FEMALE	6 INSURED'S I.D. MEDICARE AND OR MEDICAID NO (Include any letters)
	7 PATIENT'S RELATIONSHIP TO INSURED SELF SPOUSE CHILD OTHER	8 INSURED'S GROUP NO (Or Group Name)
TELEPHONE NO		

9 OTHER HEALTH INSURANCE COVERAGE - Enter Name of Policyholder and Plan Name and Address and Policy or Medical Assistance Number	10 WAS CONDITION RELATED TO A PATIENT'S EMPLOYMENT YES NO B AN AUTO ACCIDENT YES NO	11 INSURED'S ADDRESS (Street city state ZIP code)

12 PATIENT'S OR AUTHORIZED PERSON'S SIGNATURE (Read back before signing) I Authorize the Release of any Medical Information Necessary to Process this Claim and Request Payment of MEDICARE Benefits Either to Myself or to the Party Who Accepts Assignment Below SIGNED DATE	13 I AUTHORIZE PAYMENT OF MEDICAL BENEFITS TO UNDERSIGNED PHYSICIAN OR SUPPLIER FOR SERVICE DESCRIBED BELOW SIGNED-Insured or Authorized Person

PHYSICIAN OR SUPPLIER INFORMATION

14 DATE OF ILLNESS (FIRST SYMPTOM) OR INJURY (ACCIDENT) OR PREGNANCY (LMP)	15 DATE FIRST CONSULTED YOU FOR THIS CONDITION	16 HAS PATIENT EVER HAD SAME OR SIMILAR SYMPTOMS? YES NO
17 DATE PATIENT ABLE TO RETURN TO WORK	18 DATES OF TOTAL DISABILITY FROM THROUGH	DATES OF PARTIAL DISABILITY FROM THROUGH
19 NAME OF REFERRING PHYSICIAN OR OTHER SOURCE (e g public health agency)		20 FOR SERVICES RELATED TO HOSPITALIZATION GIVE HOSPITALIZATION DATES ADMITTED DISCHARGED
21 NAME & ADDRESS OF FACILITY WHERE SERVICES RENDERED (If other than home or office)		22 WAS LABORATORY WORK PERFORMED OUTSIDE YOUR OFFICE? YES NO CHARGES

23 DIAGNOSIS OR NATURE OF ILLNESS OR INJURY RELATE DIAGNOSIS TO PROCEDURE IN COLUMN D BY REFERENCE TO NUMBERS 1 2 3 ETC OR DX CODE

1
2
3
4

24 A DATE OF SERVICE	B PLACE OF SERVICE	C FULLY DESCRIBE PROCEDURES MEDICAL SERVICES OR SUPPLIES FURNISHED FOR EACH DATE GIVEN PROCEDURE CODE IDENTIFY (EXPLAIN UNUSUAL SERVICES OR CIRCUMSTANCES)	D DX CODE (ID)	E CHARGES	

25 SIGNATURE OF PHYSICIAN OR SUPPLIER (I certify that the statements on the reverse apply to this bill and are made a part hereof) SIGNED DATE	26 ACCEPT ASSIGNMENT (GOVERNMENT CLAIMS ONLY) (SEE BACK) YES NO 30 YOUR SOCIAL SECURITY NO	27 TOTAL CHARGE	28 AMOUNT PAID	29 BALANCE DUE
		31 PHYSICIAN'S OR SUPPLIER'S NAME ADDRESS ZIP CODE & TELEPHONE NO		
32 YOUR PATIENT'S ACCOUNT NO	33 YOUR EMPLOYER I D NO			
		I D NO		

● PLACE OF SERVICE CODES

1 - (IH) - INPATIENT HOSPITAL	4 - (IH) - PATIENT'S HOME	7 - (NH) - NURSING HOME	O - (OL) OTHER LOCATIONS
2 - (OH) - OUTPATIENT HOSPITAL	5 - DAY CARE FACILITY (PSY)	8 - (SNF) - SKILLED NURSING FACILITY	A - (IL) - INDEPENDENT LABORATORY
3 - O) - DOCTOR'S OFFICE	6 - NIGHT CARE FACILITY (PSY)	9 - AMBULANCE	B - OTHER MEDICAL SURGICAL FACILITY

OP-408   APPROVED BY AMA COUNCIL ON MEDICAL SERVICE 8-74

Figure 3. Medicare claim form

```
          EXPLANATION OF MEDICARE BENEFITS

Provider:      Dr. Robert L. Boothe
Provider No:   056272100
Date:          12-01-83
```

Beneficiary Name	H.I.C. Number	I.C. Number	Service Code
Reeve, Janice	059-01-8463-A	08-83-032-304-49-0	0874

When	Place and Type	Amount Billed	Amount Approved	Action/Remark Codes
08-01-83	0 1	640.00	600.00	Claim Total

Amount to Annual Deductible	Claim Balance Payable at 80%	Medicare Payment per Claim	Amount to be Paid by Patient per Claim
0.00	600.00	480.00	120.00

Figure 4. Explanation of benefits

The second point deals with the difference, if Medicare didn't approve your full fee. We customarily would charge $640—but Medicare assigned $600. That amount is lost, but you shouldn't just forget about it. It should be shown on your books as an adjustment, to maintain the sanctity of your audit trail. Technically it should be entered as an adjustment on the day you receive the check from Medicare, as follows:

12/01/83 Charge Adjustment—Mandated Fee Schedule $40.00

Otherwise, your accounts won't be very convincing with amounts forgotten at random places without explanation. It might be very important later on to be able to show the Internal Revenue Service, your bank, or even Medicare's own auditors how consistent you've been in your charges. It might also be of interest in your own profitability analysis to see what it's really costing you to work with Medicare.

FINALLY THE PROBLEM!

After that demonstration of how the Medicare claim process works, you may be thinking you see the problem. "It's all the paperwork, right? You're going to recommend a computer as an automatic form printer, right?"

Nope. A computer would indeed be very helpful there, but that's not third-party tracking. The purpose of the data manager (computer or human) is to catch errors and omissions by the third parties. Our entire example just shows how Medicare works when it's working well. The three-month delay in payments, the paperwork and red tape, the hassle of looking up codes—they're all part of the normal price you pay to treat patients on Medicare. The problem arises when you and Medicare disagree.

I should point out that my own awareness of the problem came from Dr. Robert Boothe, a leading orthopedic surgeon in Nyack, New York. He and his staff, Pat Fazio and Helen Gorman, were very helpful in providing examples of what can go wrong.

The simplest case is a data entry error. Dr. Boothe's staff showed me several cases where a procedure code came back differently on the Explanation of Benefits report than what was originally submitted. In one case a 9020 code (first visit by a patient) ended up as a 9021 (subsequent visit). In another, an X-ray of the upper arm (as a check for bone cancer) was handled as if it was a fractured wrist. A third error changed one X-ray (7252) to a cheaper one (7266).

After each such error, a "Doctor's Claim Inquiry" form was sent to Medicare. This form is, fortunately, a simple one. It requires only the HIC number, the IC number, and a description of the error in plain English. Medicare has almost always acknowledged the error in simple cases like these—and paid the differences with only another month's delay.

Realize that those errors occurred even though the claims were "precoded." That is, the procedure codes were entered, not just descriptions of the procedures. The conversion of descriptions to codes is another breeding ground for mistakes. Yet another simple foul–up is forgetting to enter one or more treatments out of a series.

In addition to these simple errors, there are the more difficult-to-resolve *disagreements* between you and the agency. One doctor in the Midwest was surprised to find one of his claims refused on the basis that his quoted fee was far beyond what was normal and customary. His surprise arose from the fact that the previous five claims for the same procedure and the same amount had been paid without a hitch. The doctor took the dispute to court and won, largely because he had kept excellent records of his past dealings with the agency.

Dr. Boothe had a similar disagreement over the case of an unfortunate elderly woman who had broken her hip in a fall; a few weeks later she broke her other hip in another fall. Medicare insisted for a remarkably long time that the second treatment was a continuation of the first one and had already been paid.

ASHTON·TATE ■

Disagreements can arise over the meanings of the codes. This is aggravated by the existence of several minor variations on the same "standard" set. In New York the CPT codes are used by the workman's compensation board, in the state regulations on no-fault insurance, and Medicaid. But each agency has a slightly different listing of codes and each listing is updated at different time intervals!

Incidentally, all the errors found by Dr. Boothe had the effect of reducing the amount approved by Medicare, and in turn increasing the amounts due from the patients. That's not just a coincidence, of course. The agency's admitted policy is to resolve all uncertainties by selecting the code with the lowest fee.

There's another advantage to keeping the procedure codes in a computerized database, even though we didn't emphasize it here. The codes are changing constantly! In New York, for example, Medicare had planned to switch the entire code book over to CPT in January 1984. That attempt at standardization will probably be helpful in the long run, but the transition period will be a "doozy." Another change contemplated for the future is a classification by diagnosis rather than by procedure. Keeping your codes in a computerized database will make it much easier for you to adjust to these sweeping changes. You'll only have to revise the database once and your office will be back on track.

THE SOLUTION

Dr. Boothe's office is using primarily a manual tracking system at present. As claims are mailed, the claim number, procedures, fees, and date of mailing are entered onto a large sheet of paper. One such sheet is kept for each patient. Later, when the third party's settlement arrives, the date, approved amounts, and approved codes are copied onto the same sheet of paper. It's then an easy task to look for all the problems we've discussed: mismatched codes, forgotten procedures, large discrepancies between charged fees and approved amounts. The office also expends the same effort in tracking cases where the *patient* is the one in danger of losing money when

ASHTON·TATE ■

Assignment was not accepted. (The primary paperwork goes to the patient in this case, but the office gets a copy of the explanation.) Some errors have meant differences of over $1,000 to the patients. Without this help, it is unlikely that the patients would know how to get the error resolved, or even to know that an error had occurred.

A typical sheet of "tracking paper" in Dr. Boothe's manual system is a wide sheet organized like the one in Figure 5. The last two lines show examples we covered above. The "status" column indicates whether or not the doctor accepted assignment.

The methods in this office are a good demonstration of the right way to approach data management: understand the problem first. Attack it manually to make sure you know what the basic procedure is and what types of data need to be kept. (This office discovered, for example, that the long Medicare claim number was too cumbersome for manual tracking. They now assign a simple four-digit sequential number to all their claims, and simply write that number on the retained copy. That's the first column of the tracking sheet.)

After the initial work, you may find that the manual system is adequate. But if the staff complains about the paperwork, if the reports you want to see take hours to do by hand, if you find yourself talking about what you'll add to the system as soon as you get time—then computerize.

In Dr. Boothe's case, that time has come. The paperwork is unquestionably an extra burden: the tracking sheet, inquiry letters, claims, and even the letters sent to the patients to explain what the Explanation of Benefits really means. There are some questions that just aren't easy to answer with manual help, especially those concerning what hasn't happened yet ("Show me all the claims that haven't been paid in more than three months"), and those that group all the patients together ("Have any of the approved fees varied significantly over the last year?").

The automation of the method should proceed smoothly, because everyone in the office feels comfortable

Our Claim	Our Proc Code	Charged Fee	M'care Code	Submissn Date	EOB Rec'd	Final Code	Approved Fee	Status	Payable at 80%	Due from Patient	Rec'd M'care	Rec'd Patient	Adjustment
1626	20010	1800.00	1007	12/15/82	3/14/83	1007	1500.00	A/A	1200.00	300.00	1200.00		300.00
1627	90260	350.00		12/16/82	3/04/83	9001	204.40	A/A	163.52	40.88	163.52		145.60
1807	90260	300.00		01/31/83	3/28/83	9001	0.00	A/A	0.00				104.00
1809	90260	250.00		02/07/83	3/28/83	9001	146.00	A/A	116.80	29.20	116.80	29.20	+0.00
2212	27506	640.00	0874	08/01/83	12/01/83	0874	600.00	A/A	480.00	120.00	480.00		!!!!!
2215	7252	55.00	7252	08/04/83	12/01/83	7266	18.40	A/A	14.72		14.72		

Figure 5. Tracking sheet

with it already. Here's our outline of the procedure as it will probably look on the computer. It splits naturally into three separate tasks.

Procedure for Third-Party Tracking

1. Claim Entry (after each visit or series of visits)
   - Enter the procedure codes (standard CPT codes or your own internal ones) to the patient's record.
   - If the patient's insurance carrier is one that uses those standard codes, the entry job is finished.
   - But if the carrier uses nonstandard codes, look up each one in a conversion table.
     - If any of the conversions are ambiguous (more than one possible match or no exact match), show a list of the closest matches and allow a choice. (The user should be able to postpone this choice until later, if there's only time for quick entry now.)
2. Payment Entry (when the check or any explanation is received)
   - Enter the data from the Explanation of Benefits form just as it's received: claim number, approved codes, number of services, amount billed, amount approved, amount paid. Also enter the check number and amount.
   - Compare each payment with the claim information previously entered into each patient's record.
   - Print an inquiry letter automatically if any of these errors are found:
     - Approved code doesn't match the submitted code.
     - Procedures are skipped in a series.
     - A late payment that should have borne interest, doesn't.
     - Calculations are incorrect, due to an arithmetic error (unlikely) or a disagreed deductible.
   - For less obvious problems, print a list for later review by the doctor:

- Difference between a charged amount and approved amount is more than 30 percent.
- Procedure is disallowed (zero approved).
- For all patients whose claims had no problems:
  - Print a bill for the proper amount.
  - Print an explanatory note of how the amount was determined.
  - Enter the proper adjustment (the unapproved part of the fee) into the ledger as a write-off.
- For all claims which had problems and on which we did not accept assignment, put a reminder on the review list to call the patient. (Those patients have received a confusing letter and a small check, and they need reassurance.)

3. Periodic Housecleaning and Reports (upon demand, weekly or monthly)
- Print the forms for all claims not yet submitted.
- Print a list of all old claims not yet acted upon (past three months) and all old inquiry letters (past one month).
- Print a report of all old patient receivables (bills not paid for three months) for decision on whether to collect or write off.
- When desired, print a history for any patient: all procedures and fees between any two specified dates. (Primarily for documenting complaints to an agency.)
- When desired, print a history for any procedure code or range of codes: charged fees, approved fees.

SUMMARY

Physicians can definitely benefit from a systematic approach to their accounts receivable, whether the system is manual or computerized. The prevalence of third-party payments and the attendant paperwork, however, tilt the scales strongly in favor of a computer. For offices which handle a lot of third-party work, the ability to do away with forms altogether in the near future is a strong attraction. The exchange of claim data in machine-readable

ASHTON·TATE ■

form or by Electronic Claim Submission will greatly reduce errors and delays in payment.

But for now, until the "golden age" of fast error-free payment arrives, a computer can perform a valuable tracking service. Quickly and tirelessly, it can look over all the claims and explanations of benefits and catch all the obvious errors and even the debatable ones. In response to the obvious errors, the computer can automatically print inquiry letters. The debatable ones you'll have to review, but at least you'll have a neat, condensed list to work from.

Notes

1. As originally described in "Computer Cure for a Doctor's Dilemma" by Mike Barlow, in the April 1983 issue of *Personal Computing*.
2. From the article "Integrated Telecommunications in the Doctor's Office" by Jerry Robinson and John Stuppy, in *Computer Dealer* magazine, December 1982.
3. You may be surprised to hear me admitting that computers make mistakes. Actually they don't, not often enough to be noticeable. But remember that a data manager isn't only a computer. It's a multi-component system, with the majority of the components being people. The errors almost always occur when the information is passing through human hands. When someone in your office fills out an insurance claim manually, one of the numbers may be illegible. When the data is entered into the company's computer (by a keypunch operator who's bored with looking at the same numbers all day long), mistakes are often made.
4. From the fourth edition of the *Current Procedural Terminology*, published by the American Medical Association, 535 N. Dearborn, Chicago, Ill. 60610.

ASHTON·TATE ■

Chapter Five

Dentists

Of all the professions in this book, dentists have the clearest justification for a computerized office system. The paperwork load in a dental office, at least in a profitable one, is staggering. Even if the computer is used only for form handling, like an automatic typewriter with memory, it will prove its worth in the hours saved filling out insurance claims, precertification forms, statements, reminder letters, and Medicare/Medicaid forms.

Dentists, as a class, are more willing to handle insurance forms on the patient's behalf than are M.D.'s. I'm not sure how that tradition started, but a dentist is less likely to ask the patient to pay out of pocket and then file the claim on his own. A major reason may be "precertification," which allows the dentist to determine in advance of the treatments how much the company will pay. That makes the payment faster and more secure than billing the patient.

We'll see three good examples of *form handling* in this chapter: precertifications, recall letters, and reminder letters. Of course, dentists also need to watch their *accounts receivable*, that universal application we described in Chapter Three.

ASHTON·TATE ■

Client list management is a necessity. In fact, the recall procedure we're about to discuss is just a specialized form of list manipulation, with an emphasis on calendar dates. Another instance is the birthday list procedure, like our first simple illustration. If you're a dentist who treats children, an annual birthday card can help cement your relationship.

Profitability analysis (Chapter Three) is another application shared by dentists with other professionals. A regular review of how much money is being brought in by each class of service—restorative, diagnostic, surgical, and so on—can reveal where you should add more capability or cut back. The overall objective, of course, is to achieve the maximum return from the fixed office space and the fixed number of days in a month. If the analysis is broken down by individual provider in a multiple provider clinic, it can help pinpoint where each member should specialize.

A corollary of this capability is *income analysis*. In a large clinic, you might want to apportion each provider's salary according to some agreed-upon rule based on production. (A "provider" can be a dentist, hygienist, radiologist, or other income producer.) A simple rule might be for a percentage of the income actually brought in, where the exact percentage depends on years with the clinic and individual negotiation. If you'll look back at the profitability report illustrated in Chapter Three, you'll see that that rule would be easy to add; all the hard work of classifying the income has already been done. With a few extra seconds, the computer could keep a running total of each provider's production, and at the end of the report apply the income rule and print each salary. Or print the salaries on individual pieces of paper if you don't want them publicized. Come to think of it, at this point it would be trivial merely to print the checks. The information is all there and just needs to be rearranged in a format to suit the check—a case of form handling. But that's getting into a whole new application—payroll—which isn't really a big benefit unless the clinic has ten or more providers. If you get that far you'll also want the

ASHTON·TATE ■

computer to keep track of taxes, social security, and W-2 forms.

Getting back to the income analysis, I'd like to make one more point. Approach this subject with caution and tact. If one of the providers feels that he or she is being watched by "Big Brother Computer," this will only cause problems. If that's the case, don't go any further than the profitability analysis, and even then don't break down each person's production. Treat the clinic as a unit, as one big provider. A good flexible computer system should let you do that. On the other hand, if all parties agree to the income analysis idea, it can avoid arguments later. For example, one of the providers might feel the need to lighten his work load for a while. He can do it without feeling that he's letting everyone else down as it's already been decided what the effect will be on his share of the income.

A dental office may run into as much third-party red tape as the physicians did in Chapter Four. Medicare, Medicaid, electronic claims submission, third-party tracking—they're all candidates for a dental office manager's chores. Fortunately for dentists, the American Dental Association seems to have done a good job of standardizing the procedure codes and claim forms, and getting the third parties to agree to the standards. Thus, dentists don't have all the headaches covered in Chapter Four; converting codes between agencies is seldom necessary.

Those are the commonly shared applications, but each profession has some requirements that set it apart from the others. For dentists, those special needs are patient recall and insurance precertification. That's not to say that other professionals can't benefit from the use of these procedures (as evidenced by the increasing use of patient recall by physicians), but they're the extra capabilities a data manager must have to be useful to dentists. We'll also give some thought to appointment tracking, which is to some extent applicable to physicians and lawyers.

ASHTON·TATE ■

The best way to demonstrate the key points of a patient recall application, as I've been preaching throughout this book, is to analyze a good manual system. The best recall system I've seen in operation is that of Dr. Robert N. Needle and Dr. Franklyn D. Church, who run a very successful office in the middle of Manhattan. The data managers in this system (definitely human and much more attractive than computers) are Casey Kretmar and Jane Fern.

The recall procedure practiced by this office is, in a nutshell, to send a written reminder to each patient when it's time to arrange for preventive maintenance.

Whoops, my computer background is showing—I should say for "examination and prophylaxis." Preventive maintenance is a phrase usually applied to machines, but the idea is the same: minor attention at regular intervals to make sure major repairs are never required. The bad thing about preventive maintenance, from a marketing viewpoint, is that the customer is asked to make an investment *before* there's a clearly felt need. Computer companies invariably resolve this dilemma by providing a "service contract," a payment in advance as insurance against serious downtime. Automobile dealers ask you to bring your car in at regular mileage checkpoints, sometimes threatening the negation of a warranty if you ignore the advice. Dentists, however, can't use these approaches, or at least they haven't yet. If a dentist waited for patients to bring their teeth in every 10,000 chews, he'd end up "as lonely as the Maytag repairman."

The dentist must accept the job of remembering when the patients should come in. Many patients, unless someone does the remembering for them, would never see the dentist until they were reminded by a toothache.

In its simplest form, patient recall is merely a reminder six months after the patient's last cleaning, the last prophylaxis date ("prophy" for short). This is a straightforward example of client list management, a refugee from Chapter Three. In your homegrown database, you've kept personal data (name and address) and transaction data

PATIENT RECALL

(last prophy date). The structured-English outline is as follows:

Basic Patient Recall Procedure

Look through each patient's folder to find the last prophy date. (In database parlance, get the contents of the Last-Prophy field from each patient record.)

Add six months to get the Recommended Date for another cleaning.

If the Recommended Date lies within the near future,

Write the name, address, telephone, and Last-Prophy date on a list.

Make a note in the patient's record that he or she has been called.

Continue until the end of the patient file.

Put away the patient file.

Send cards or letters (or phone calls) to everyone on the list.

That vague reference to the near future should be replaced by whatever time span makes sense for your office. It should begin far enough in the future to allow time for the letter to arrive and for the appointment to be made (say a week from today). When it ends depends on how often you repeat this procedure—for example, every two weeks. So, the "near future" might be "between one week and three weeks from today."

The choice of cards, letters, or telephone calls is a matter of style. Drs. Needle and Church cater to a fairly sophisticated and busy clientele (New York City-ites), so they send individually typed, personalized letters. Cards are more typical.

Follow-up. Another step in the outline is to leave a note in each patient record that the recall has actually been made. The notation might be as simple as a paper clip in a reserved spot on the file. Without it you won't be really sure, when you follow up with another recall, whether the patient is ignoring your advice or whether it's your oversight. It will also serve as a placemarker, if you don't have time to search through the entire file in one sitting (as is usually the case). It's especially helpful if more than one person in the office is assisting in the task. Just don't forget to remove the paper clip when the patient does come in for the next cleaning.

Chances are some of your clients won't respond right away. As you're going through the file, you'll come across paper clips still in place representing patients who have been reminded but haven't come in yet. Let's be fair—they might be on vacation. Give them three months to make an appointment. We'll want to add a few extra steps in our outline:

Follow-Up Enhancement
If a patient has been recalled but hasn't responded:
Add three more months to the Last-Prophy Date.
If that Second-Notice Date lies within the near future,
Write the name, address, and Last-Prophy Date on a second list.
Make a note of the second attempt (two clips).
Send appropriately worded letters to the second list.

This follow-up could obviously be extended for as many notices as you like, but three is a reasonable limit. After that you can quit trying, or perhaps do what the office of Church-and-Needle does. Send a polite but firm letter to the effect that you'll be happy to transfer the patient's records to the other dentist they'll be seeing.

Extra Control: Why and How Often. The recall method, as it stands now, is fine for many offices but it might not be everything you want. If you have a large, loyal group of patients you need more flexibility, a finer adjustment on the system. You find yourself asking questions like, "Who's due for periodontal treatment in the months of July and August?" (Your periodontal specialist is going on an extended vacation.) Maybe six months between cleanings isn't accurate for everyone.

The office of Drs. Church and Needle classifies recalls by the kind of service that's needed in the next checkup, the recall *reason*. An EX is a visit for an exam and X-ray, a PX is a prophylaxis, and a CMX is a complete mouth X-ray. They also keep track of the duration of the appointment needed, in quarter-hour units. Thus, an entry in their manual system looks like this:

Name	Reason	Last One	Next One	Units Needed
John Doe	PX	06/01/83	12/01/83	3
	EX	06/01/83	06/01/84	2
	CMX	06/01/82	06/01/84	2

This tells them more than just to remind John Doe to call for a cleaning around December 1. It also makes it easy to remember, when he does call, to allow 45 minutes for it.

FREQUENCY

You'll notice that the interval between visits varies with each of the reasons. Typically, a cleaning (PX) is required every six months, an exam (EX) is needed every 12 months, and a complete X-ray (CMX) every 24. We might call that the recall *frequency*. But the number doesn't have to be a constant! Each person's mouth is different, so the frequency is dependent on the individual.

When we start talking about "variable recall frequencies," you may think we're creating complications for no good reason. However, we're justified because by letting a computer handle the extra complexity, we can make things easier for the human staff (Casey and Jane). We'll require the computer to remember three recall frequencies for each patient, one for each of the recall reasons. Then, in the course of our normal daily transaction entries, the computer can be on the lookout for cleanings, X-rays, and exams. We need an example. Let's say we enter a transaction like this for that same patient:

Name	Date	Procedure Code	Amount
John Doe	12/15/83	1110	$35.00

The computer can then "think" through with the following logic: "That 1110 code is a prophylaxis. So John Doe finally came in for the appointment we recommended!

About time, too... Well, I'll just change the Last-Prophy-laxis-Date in his record to 12/15/83, so we won't forget to remind him next year."

That's all that is required: just an update of the Last Date fields whenever one of the three recall procedures (cleaning, X-rays, exam) is performed. It can be done quickly enough so that we won't even notice it while we're entering transactions. The time saving lies in the fact that we no longer have to manually enter the next-visit date. The computer will be able to figure it out by adding the appropriate frequency to the last date.

I should point out one underlying assumption here. The recall frequencies for each patient, once they're estab-lished, are assumed not to vary with time. They're stable. If John Doe should come in every eight months for a cleaning, that'll be the right cycle for him forever, or at least for several years. If we have to enter a new frequency after every visit, obviously we haven't saved any steps over the manual method.

One more refinement is required. Occasionally you want to see a patient for some once-only reason. You performed some emergency procedure for Mrs. Brown and want to see her again in three months to monitor her progress. Or Mr. Baker changed jobs and won't have dental insurance coverage for a year. You will want to see him then.

To avoid confusion, let's call the three common recall reasons (EX, PX,CMX) the *regular* reasons. (The word "regular" is ideal in either of its two meanings: (1) usual and customary, or (2) occurring in a stable, periodic cycle.) Then these one-timers are *special* recall reasons. What we're really designing here is a tickler file, a simple little reminder system for arbitrary dates and arbitrary reasons.

To handle the special recalls, we have only to add one more date and reason to the patient record. We don't need a frequency since the recall won't come up again and there's no Date-Procedure-Last-Given to add to. The special recall date is the one day we want to see the patient again.

Finishing the Design. Speaking of patient records, we haven't yet discussed how to include the paper clip markers of our manual system. Each type of recall needs an extra little field where we can make a note that we've notified the patient. The best approach is to put a numeral in that spot that corresponds to the number of paper clips: a "0" means not recalled since the last visit, a "1" means one notification but no return visit yet, and so on. I'll call this new item the "Notified" field.

The patient record, then, includes 16 new fields to support our recall system:

Name and other personal data as usual.

The regular recall types:

```
Last-EX-Date,   EX-Frequency,   EX-Notified,   EX-Units
Last-PX-Date,   PX-Frequency,   PX-Notified,   PX-Units
Last-CMX-Date,  CMX-Frequency,  CMX-Notified,  CMX-Units
```

And one optional special recall date:

```
Special-Date, Special-Reason, Special-
Notified, Special-Units.
```

The Special-Reason field is just a reminder to ourselves of why we wanted to see the patient. It could be anything from a single letter ("P" for Periodontal) to a sentence.

With that much information we can perform some pretty complicated client list management. (You have, of course, read Chapters Two and Three, so you're comfortable with all this talk of fields and records and list management.) "Show me all patients of Dr. Needle who will be recalled in the next six weeks for exams." "Show me all the special recalls for periodontal work in the next three months." With a computer to search through the files for us, we can ask questions like that without overloading our staff.

Here's the outline with all the enhancements.

Super Patient Recall Procedure

Specify which recalls you wish to see: what range of dates

(the near future you care about), and which reasons (special reasons or just the regular ones, or all).

Taking each patient's record:

If the Special-Reason is one of the reasons specified,

If the Special-Date is within the near future,

If three notices haven't already been sent,

Recall the patient.*

For each of the three regular reasons (if they were specified):

If three notices haven't already been sent:

Calculate:

Last-Date + Frequency + (Notified x 3 months) = Return Date

(An example: if this patient's last cleaning was on 02/01/83, and his proper frequency is one cleaning every eight months, but he has already been notified twice: 02/01/83 + 8 months + (2 x 3 months) = 04/01/84 So he needs to be reminded one last time if 04/01/84 is in the near future.)

If that Return Date lies within the specified near future:

Recall the patient.*

Continue until the end of the patient file.

Put away the patient file.

Send cards or letters to everyone on the list, appropriately phrased for each recall type and reason.

*I merely wrote "Recall the patient" in two places to avoid repeating a sequence of steps. Here are the steps to be followed in each of those places:

Mark that the patient has been notified by adding 1 to the Notified field.

Write on the list:

Name, Address, and Phone,

Recall Reason (cleaning, X-rays, exam, or specific reason),

ASHTON·TATE ■

Recall Report For All Reasons

12/01/83 to 12/31/83

Name, Address, Phone	Reason	Units	Notif'n	Last Date
Carl Downs	Exam	2	2	06/12/83
2000 Syrup Hill	X-rays	1	2	12/20/81
Yorick, NY 10598				
(914) 555-2372				
Janice Reeve	Bridge	4	1	
1600 Pennsylvania Ave.				
Putnam Valley, NY 10579				
(914) 555-1212				

**Figure 1. Recall report listing all patients who should be reminded to
schedule an appointment**

Units to allow for appointment,
Notified Level (1, 2, or 3),
Last-Date.

In programmer's terms, I've put those common steps into a subroutine, a miniature procedure on the side that I can make use of more than once.

The Results. I'll end this section by showing you the kind of reports you might get as answers to your inquiries. A report you'd see for the request, "Show me all the patients who should be recalled in December for any reason" is shown in Figure 1.

That's the report you'll want if you intend to use the telephone for your contacts. All the information you need for an efficient call is there. If the patient decides to schedule an appointment right then, you know which procedures and how much time to schedule.

If, on the other hand, you prefer to send letters, that report isn't enough. You'd like to avoid retyping all those names and addresses if possible. For this we pull out our trusty word processor from Chapter Three to merge the names into a nice letter and print them all automatically. To do that, we ask our data manager to spit out the same list of names to an intermediate file (that's what we called "printing to disk," remember) where our word processor can get at it. Although it's not actually printed, it contains the following information:

Carl Downs
2000 Syrup Hill
Yorick, NY 10598
Exam
1
06/12/83
X-rays
1
12/20/81
.
.
.

ASHTON·TATE ■

From that list, the merge capability of our word processor will automatically produce a letter like the one shown in Figure 2.

The idea behind an insurance precertification or preauthorization (or just "precert" as it's also called) isn't hard to understand, but few patients are aware of it. The dentist is unique among professionals in that he has the time to perform an examination first, to find out what services are needed, and then have a few weeks before those services are actually scheduled to be performed. Of course, even dentists don't always have this luxury—emergencies do occur. But in the typical case there's an examination, perhaps a couple of restorations in the next visit, then more treatment if necessary in another visit. There's time to alert the insurance company as to what's intended.

After the exam, a precertification form is filled out with the planned services. An example is shown below. It's exactly the same form as the standard claim that's filed after the work is done, with two differences: the dates of the procedures aren't filled in yet (since they haven't been done yet), and there is a small box to be checked at the top to indicate that this is a precertification request. (Another example of the advanced state of standardization accomplished by the ADA). An example of a precertification form is shown in Figure 3.

The insurance company evaluates this form, checking things like: is the patient really a member of the plan, are the procedures covered, have they been done before? It replies to your office that some or all of the work is approved. The "payoff" comes after the services are performed. When you send the real claim, you remind the company of the prior approval by including the claim number from the precertification. That avoids the approval step, and the payment is sent at once.

In addition to the speedup in payment, the precert procedure catches potential non-payment problems in advance. If the patient isn't really insured (usually an honest mistake), you'll know it up front. You'll also know

ASHTON·TATE ■

Janice Dalton, D.D.S.
892 Avenue B
Narberth, NY 10682

Carl Downs
2000 Syrup Hill
Yorick, NY   10598

    Please call our office to arrange an appointment. You're overdue for:

        Exam   (last performed 06/12/83)
        X-rays   (last performed 12/20/810

    This is our second reminder. Please don't neglect your dental heath
any longer!

Figure 2. Computer generated reminder letter

ATTENDING DENTIST'S STATEMENT

CHECK ONE:
☒ DENTIST'S PRE-TREATMENT ESTIMATE
☐ DENTIST'S STATEMENT OF ACTUAL SERVICES

CARRIER
NAME AND ADDRESS
BLUE CROSS
3 PARK AVE.
NEW YORK, NY   10016

1 PATIENT NAME			2 RELATIONSHIP TO EMPLOYEE	3 SEX	4 PATIENT BIRTHDATE	5 IF FULL TIME STUDENT	
Jackie Q. Client			SELF ☒ SPOUSE ☐ CHILD ☐ OTHER ☐	M ☐ F ☒	MO 03 DAY 05 YEAR 50	SCHOOL	CITY

FIRST   MIDDLE   LAST

6 EMPLOYEE/SUBSCRIBER NAME
Jackie Q. Client

7 EMPLOYEE/SUBSCRIBER SOCIAL SECURITY NO.
912345678

9 NAME OF GROUP DENTAL PROGRAM

8 EMPLOYEE/SUBSCRIBER MAILING ADDRESS
987 South Park
CITY, STATE, ZIP
New York, NY   10021

10 EMPLOYER (COMPANY) NAME
IBM Corp.
EMPLOYER (COMPANY) ADDRESS
Armonk, NY

11 GROUP NUMBER 12 LOCATION(LOCAL) 13 ARE OTHER FAMILY MEMBERS EMPLOYED?
EMPLOYEE NAME   SOC. SEC. NO.

14 NAME AND ADDRESS OF EMPLOYER IN ITEM 13

15 IS PATIENT COVERED BY ANOTHER DENTAL PLAN?   DENTAL PLAN NAME   UNION LOCAL   GROUP NO.   NAME AND ADDRESS OF CARRIER

I HAVE REVIEWED THE FOLLOWING TREATMENT PLAN. I AUTHORIZE RELEASE OF ANY INFORMATION RELATING TO THIS CLAIM.

PATIENT SIGNATURE ON FILE   04/30/83
SIGNED (PATIENT, OR PARENT IF MINOR)   DATE

I HEREBY AUTHORIZE PAYMENT DIRECTLY TO THE BELOW-NAMED DENTIST OF THE GROUP INSURANCE BENEFITS OTHERWISE PAYABLE TO ME.

PATIENT SIGNATURE ON FILE   04/30/83
SIGNED (INSURED PERSON)   DATE

16 DENTIST NAME
JOHN C. DOE, D.D.S.
17 MAILING ADDRESS
123 MAIN STREET
CITY, STATE, ZIP
NEW YORK, NY   10001

18 DENTIST SOC. SEC. OR T.I.N.   19 DENTIST LICENSE NO.   20 DENTIST PHONE NO.
91-0689983 3608, NYDS:1234 (212)555-1212

21 FIRST VISIT DATE CURRENT SERIES   22 PLACE OF TREATMENT OFFICE ☐ HOSP. ☐ ECF ☐ OTHER ☐   23 RADIOGRAPHS OR MODELS ENCLOSED?   NO ☐ YES ☐   HOW MANY?

	NO	YES	IF YES, ENTER BRIEF DESCRIPTION AND DATES
24 IS TREATMENT RESULT OF OCCUPATIONAL ILLNESS OR INJURY?	XX		
25 IS TREATMENT RESULT OF AUTO ACCIDENT?			
26 OTHER ACCIDENT?	XX		
27 ARE ANY SERVICES COVERED BY ANOTHER PLAN?	XX		

28 IF PROTHESIS, IS THIS INITIAL PLACEMENT?   (IF NO, REASON FOR REPLACEMENT)   29 DATE OF PRIOR PLACEMENT

30 IS TREATMENT FOR ORTHODONTICS?   IF SERVICES ALREADY COMMENCED, ENTER   DATE APPLIANCES PLACED   MOS. TREATMENT REMAINING

IDENTIFY MISSING TEETH WITH "X"

31 EXAMINATION AND TREATMENT PLAN-LIST IN ORDER FROM TOOTH NO.1 THROUGH TOOTH NO.32 - USE CHARTING SYSTEM SHOWN

TOOTH NO. OR LETTER	SURFACE	DESCRIPTION OF SERVICE (INCLUDING X RAYS, PROPHYLAXIS, MATERIALS USED, ETC.) LINE NO.	DATE SERVICE PERFORMED MO DAY YR.	PROCEDURE NUMBER	FEE	FOR ADMINISTRATIVE USE ONLY
8	MO	ROOT CANAL, 2 CANAL		3320	210.00	

32. REMARKS FOR UNUSUAL SERVICES

I HEREBY CERTIFY THAT THE PROCEDURES AS INDICATED BY DATE HAVE BEEN COMPLETED

DATE 04/30/83

SIGNED (DENTIST)

TOTAL FEE CHARGED	
MAX ALLOWABLE	
DEDUCTIBLE	
CARRIER %	
CARRIER PAYS	
PATIENT PAYS	

Form Approved by the Council on Dental Care Programs of the A.D.A. 1975
BS-712 (9-75)

Figure 3. Precertification form

or at least have a good estimate of how much the company will pay.

The precert procedure is a good example of the extra paperwork an office bears to minimize payment problems. As a paperwork problem, it's ideal for computer solution. The computer won't complain at all at having to remember a long claim number and typing almost the same form twice.

All of us are familiar with the appointment book, that large ledger filled with little boxes for each day of the week and time of day. Every office I've been in uses one, and for good reason. It's the right tool for the job! I personally don't believe a computer can replace the manual appointment book, although I know of several computer programs that have tried. I even tried to do it myself once. The problem is that you want to see a lot of information *together*, on one page.

Let's say you want to schedule a 30-minute appointment two weeks from now. With the book you can flip to the right pages and see at a glance where the schedule's tight (no white space) and where it's loose (gaps on the page). It's obvious to you without actually reading the information. You can easily cater to all the whims of your office. (Doctor A doesn't like a full schedule on Monday morning, Doctor B would just as soon have 15 minutes slack between appointments, and so on.) A computer has trouble doing all that with the same speed. The problem is more in the field of artificial intelligence (large scale pattern recognition) than it is in the field of data management, which manipulates one small tidbit of information at a time.[1]

Hence, I don't recommend a computer for *making* appointments. But that doesn't mean it can't be a big help in tracking them, as an assistant to the book. Bear with me through an example of a typical Monday morning in the office. Pretend that all of the appointments have been made already (manually). If people weren't people, we'd have nothing more to discuss. Your patients would all

APPOINTMENTS

ASHTON·TATE ■

remember their times, never cancel, never be late, right? Hah. The phone rings. It's Mrs. Collins. She knows she has an appointment next month some time, but she's lost the little card you sent her. Could you please tell her when it is? This isn't quite what the designers of the appointment book had in mind. Now you're in computer territory. In a moment (five to 30 seconds) a computer could find the name and display the time. (While it's searching, and while you've got Mrs. Collins on the phone, it could also show you the account balance and overdue amounts.)

Then Mr. Fox calls at 10:00. He's terribly sorry, but he can't make his appointment at 2:00 today. You understand how it is, don't you? Well, whether you do or not, you have a 30-minute slot sitting idle four hours from now. The obvious thing to do is call up another patient who would love to come in today, someone who has an appointment in the next week or two for a mild toothache. Thanks to your great foresight, you entered into your computer each patient's preferences for appointment times. Now we have a simple client-list management question. "Show me all patients (names and phone numbers) who have an appointment in the next two weeks *and* who like to come in on Monday afternoons." A few phone calls, and bingo! You've just manufactured extra income out of thin air! If you earn $50 a day like this, the computer has earned its keep in under a year.

To be accurate, you haven't really brought in *new* income. You've avoided losing income, which is just as good. If you want new income, you ought to charge Mr. Fox something for cancelling his appointment on such short notice. If that's your policy, the computer can take care of all the details with little extra effort on your part. When you tell the computer that Mr. Fox's appointment has been cancelled, it can think, "That's a cancellation with less than 24 hours' notice. Our fee for that is $20. I'll just pull out the ledger (open the transactions file) and add a Cancellation Charge transaction. Then it'll automatically show up on his next statement."

A third example, a good reason for retrieving appointments after they've been made, is reminder letters. If you have a policy, as do Drs. Needle and Church, of mailing a personalized letter to a patient a week before the scheduled visit, then the computer can easily combine its list management and automatic printing capabilities and save you lots of typing. If you remind your patients by phone, the computer can still save you the effort of looking up the phone numbers. The two possibilities are the same as was covered in the section on recalls: form letters for mailing, or a condensed report for calling.

Those are illustrations of what I mean by *assisting* the appointment book. It means extra work, of course. After you've manually entered the time in the book, you have to re-enter the name and time at the computer keyboard. Whether it's worth the work depends on your practice. If your workday is packed to the brim, if every unfilled slot really is lost money, then it's probably well worth the effort.[2]

RELATED SPECIALISTS

This chapter has spoken exclusively of dentists, but I think of that as a category of specialists including orthodontists, periodontists, maxilofacial surgeons, and others. I'm well aware that many of you specialists don't agree that a "dentist" is a category. Your training and clientele is distinct enough that you don't consider yourself to be a dentist at all. But the functions you need to manage your office are similar enough to be in the same class for the purposes of this book.

There are differences in your needs, of course. Some of your procedures have been assigned a separate group of ADA codes, for example. If you're an oral surgeon, you often need to resort to an entirely different set of codes, such as the ICDA diagnostic codes used by physicians and hospitals. You'll probably find many things to interest you in the preceding chapter.

If you're an orthodontist, you probably emphasize budget plans much more in your billing. You're frequently able to plan an extensive series of visits in advance, and

ASHTON·TATE ▪

know the often sizeable magnitude of the work that will
be performed. A series of equal monthly payments is the
sensible course.

For all those specialists (surgeons, orthodontists, periodontists) for whom repeat visits are much less common
(usually consisting of only one checkup a month or two
after the treatments), the need for patient recall is slight.
A simple recall system, more like a tickler file, is helpful
for keeping track of patients who will start their treatments in the near future.

For the very same reason, close control of accounts
receivable is extremely important. If you're not careful to
maintain monthly contact with the patients who owe you
money, patients who have no other reason to think of you
again, you're liable to find yourself with more than your
share of "recalcitrants." Another aggravating factor here is
the irregularity of the charges—a large balance in a short
period of time as opposed to the steadier charges of a
general dentist.

SUMMARY

A dentist's office provides several excellent examples
where an efficient data manager (computerized or human)
can have a dramatic effect on profits. By rearranging the
daily transactions that you've been collecting a little at a
time in your homegrown database, you can have all the
following capabilities:

> Patient recall—a classic example of client list
> management, but with a little more arithmetic than
> normal in its manipulation of calendar dates. Its
> objectives are: to increase your volume, to keep the
> patients coming back, and to smooth out your cash
> flow by bringing the patients in for small regular
> visits rather than for expensive crises years apart.
> The advantages of a computer are a saving of time
> and labor in searching through the files, and the
> ability to ask more complicated questions concerning
> all the patients together at arbitrary times in the
> future.

Precertifications—standard form handling. Its objectives are to speed up payments from the insurance company and to catch non-payments before they occur. The computer simply saves you the manual labor of filling in the form twice.

Appointment tracking—list management again, when it's applied to appointments after they're made. The computer makes it easy to find patients by name, to search for a replacement to fill a short-notice cancellation, and to send reminder letters.

The other common applications—accounts receivable, profitability analysis, and general purpose inquiries into the patient records—are very important in a dental office as well.

Notes

1. It's theoretically possible to imitate the manual appointment book in a computerized data management system. I could try to display a full week's page all at once on the video screen. Then you, the user, could see the patterns just like before. Even better, you could move around the screen and fill in new appointments or change old ones, with complete freedom just as you can in the book. Sounds simple enough, but what kind of equipment do I need? The page has to be six days across. If each appointment slot needs 30 characters of space (at least!) for writing in, that's a total width of 180 characters. It will also have a separate line for every 15-minute interval from 8:00 a.m. to 5:00 p.m., let's say. That's 36 lines high, plus a few extra for titles and other auxiliary messages. We need a video screen 180 characters wide by 40 high! (If that doesn't strike you as difficult, be reminded that most video screens will handle 80 by 24. Maybe 132 by 25, or 80 by 66 in the more expensive equipment.) And it had better be a fast screen, so you can flip pages as quickly as you can by hand.

    How do I provide the freedom of movement? I can't ask the user to enter a column number and then a row number for every change of position. I'd better add a joystick or a trackball just like a video game in an arcade. By the way, here's the bill for your new system: $10,000 extra for each screen. Look at the bright side . . . you won't have to buy appointment books any more. You'll regain your investment in a few centuries.

2. Will the extra effort go away in a few years as hardware improvements are made? If large, fast video displays become commonplace (as discussed in my last note), we might be able to replace the appointment book. Or the book might remain, with the chore of re-entering the data at the keyboard eliminated. Voice input is a possibility—you'd just speak the name as you write it. Another possibility is to make the computer recognize your handwriting, although you'll undoubtedly have to print neatly for the foreseeable future. But don't forget that people's names are the most severe test of these new technologies. Even humans aren't 100 percent accurate in recognizing "Casimir Wojnilower" when they hear it or see it in writing! No, I stand by my prognostication. Appointment books will be around for a while, and touch typing will be a handy skill to have.

ASHTON·TATE ■

Chapter Six

Lawyers

Lawyers are a strange breed—at least to a computer professional. Your business is putting other people's matters in order (often with the help of meticulously worded documents), but your own records aren't always so well organized. Most of you don't have any systematic way of knowing how productive you were last year or even last month, whether your cash flow is getting better or worse, or which parts of your business are the most profitable.

Many of you already have computers in your firms, but you use them primarily for word processing. You seldom use them for data management and you rarely touch the keyboard yourself.

In other words, you're a frustration to a computer professional. Consider the following quote from someone who has been in both professions:

"If you are thinking about selling computers or word processors to lawyers, my recommendation is to forget it....I'm a lawyer selling to lawyers and know how frustrating this business is....The law office is an ideal place for automation. Therefore, many lawyers have obtained equipment early in the game. They were sold on the

ASHTON·TATE ■

idea of office automation before it was
perfected. They bought computers
before they were user friendly, before
the prices came down, and before
special software was available. And, they
got burned.
Attorneys have their own ways of keeping records. They make notes on the
back of envelopes, on paper napkins, or
in their heads. Then, at billing time,
they scramble around for hours trying
to put the information together."[1]

Well, let's pretend we don't know any better and barge
right on, starry-eyed with the wonders of automation. The
problems and bottlenecks will become apparent soon
enough. As I've said several times before, the objective of
this book is to get you thinking about how you manage
your office, about where you can increase your profits—
regardless of whether your data managers are humans or
computers.

You have as great a need as the other professionals, if
not greater, for tracking your *accounts receivable*. After all,
doctors, dentists, and pharmacists do occasionally get paid
in cash at the conclusion of a service. That almost never
happens to you. The vast majority of your income starts
as a receivable.

Client list management, the other major application we
discussed in Chapter Three, is also a natural. (One of our
examples was a lawyer's inquiry: "Show me all the clients
who had a will prepared last year in New York.") That
wealth of information you've built up on your clients will
be a gold mine if you ever decide to run for a political
office, which is something lawyers are much more prone
to do than our other professionals. Pretend you're running
for town justice, for example. You have your own homegrown database of clients, names of people already
convinced of your integrity. You can send a letter to all
your friends in voting District 9, urging them to get out
the vote.

Another good way to use client list management is to bring together clients with mutual interests. Your clients often come to you for financial and investment advice. Suppose you advised John Doe to diversify his portfolio by selling his lakeside lot; he's naturally going to ask if you know anyone who'd like to buy it. If you've been keeping conscientious notes over the years on every person who likes to invest in real estate, you can help Mr. Doe, and yourself. If your client list is on a computer, you'll just say, "Show me all clients and phone numbers who have an interest in real estate." That'll take less than a minute. (Sort of a computer dating service, but based on mutual financial interests rather than mutual hobbies.) As I recommended in Chapter Three, it helps to imagine in advance the kinds of questions you'll want to ask. That will show you what items you'll want stored in your files, i.e., the fields in your database. For this question you'll want a field to remember investment interests.

Form handling is another need you share with other professionals. Many of the documents you prepare for your clients are fairly well standardized. Over the years, you've developed your own forms; you know they work well and you can save your client time and money in many cases just by filling in the blanks. However, this is only a borderline example of data management, in that you seldom generate more than one of any given form at one time. Word processing systems are ideal for this kind of work: form letters, boiler plate documents, and last-minute replacement of specific names and addresses.

But many of your data management needs are unique. The most important single factor that sets you apart is your emphasis on time. Many of your services are billed on a time basis. That, in turn, affects your receivables and the way you handle funds in escrow. The first application we'll examine in depth is *timekeeping and billing*.

Deadlines are another manifestation of time. You have to remember to file briefs by a certain day, to pay annual patent fees, to renew trademarks, to do something before that statute of limitations runs out, and so on. *Calendar control* is the second unique problem we'll look at.

Finally, lawyers are unique in the number of documents that must be processed. In a complicated case or lawsuit, there are often more references, citations, and depositions than one individual can possibly comprehend as a unified whole. The best example of this was the recently-dropped dispute between the Justice Department and IBM, in which IBM reputedly delivered documents to court by the truck-load! In a case like that, no one person can remember which references support or disprove any particular point of fact. A computer can help by virtue of its ability to search quickly through text. That's the third and last application we'll examine, a *litigation support* system.

I'm going to put myself in the place of your legal assistant or secretary. (Most of you lawyers have trouble imagining *yourself* sitting at a computer or even entering data into an organized bookkeeping system, so I'll save you that discomfort by casting myself as your secretary.) My first job in the morning is to make sense of the scraps of paper you (the attorney) left on my desk at the end of the previous day. That's the way we've done things in this office ever since I gave up trying to persuade you to write your time and expenses on a single sheet. So, you can follow your natural tendency to scribble on whatever slip of paper you may have in hand at the moment, and empty your pockets onto my desk at the day's end.

Let's see, here's an envelope with a note on the back. "Conference with Abe Sturms. Hour and a half." Here's a matchbook bearing "Tolls and parking $8.50, Smith hearing." And a business card with "20 minutes phone call to Stevens" written on the back. Finally a napkin with "Appeared in court, Spinner divorce, 9:00 to 12:00. Lunch, my treat, $22."

I'll enter those items onto a single sheet of paper, a time and expense journal. (See Figure 1.)

The "Type of Service" column specifies what was actually done. We need to keep track of that for the client's

TIMEKEEPING AND BILLING

ASHTON·TATE ■

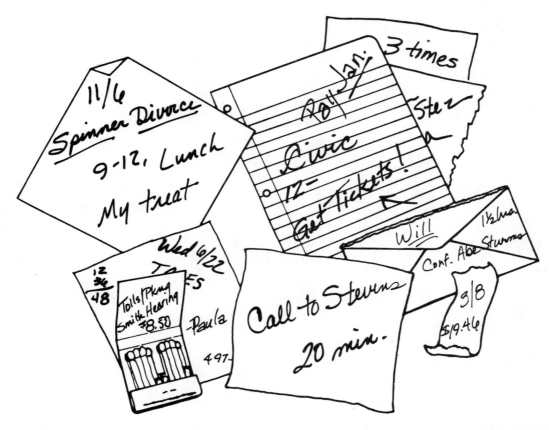

Attorney:	E.S. Samalin				Date: 10-7-83
Client or Case	Type of Service	Time, hh:mm	Expense Type	Expense Amount	Comments
Sturms	Conference	1:30			
Smith			Tolls	8.50	To hearing.
Stevens	Conference	:20			Phone call.
Spinner	Trial	3:00	Meal-NB	22.00	Trial lunch.

Figure 1. Daily time and expenses journal

bill at the end of the month, among other reasons. Typical entries might be Depositions, Hearings, Document Preparation, and Office Management.[2]

The "Expense Type" column has a similar purpose, but for clarifying expenses rather than services. Those identifications will show up on the client's monthly statement. At least they will if they're billable. The lunch you so graciously paid for won't look so gracious if you reverse the charges. That's why the entry is "Meal-NB" (NonBillable), to remind your billing system not to include this expense. Why put it in the journal at all? Because it's for your income tax return, as well as your own information.

The "comments" column is there for clarity, to make your records readable years later when you've forgotten the details of the case.

DAILY JOURNAL

Step One: The Daily Journal. I know from experience (in my role as secretary) that you don't always remember everything that should be entered. Indeed, I can tell from this simple journal that you've left out a few things. If I were to take your notes as gospel, I'd have to believe that you drove to the Smith hearing but didn't spend any time there.

In Chapter Three we discussed a clear audit trail, and the use of a daily journal for making corrections before posting to the real books. This daily time and expense journal will serve the same purpose. I bring it, neatly typed, into your office for you to peruse with your morning coffee. (Of course, I was at work an hour before you got here.) The events of the preceding day are still fresh enough in your mind so that you're able to fill in the missing information. You pencil in the 45 minutes you spent at the Smith hearing.

I pick up the corrected journal ten minutes later when I bring in your list of appointments for the day. It takes a couple of minutes for me to make the corrections in the permanent time and expense file, and yesterday is put to rest. Wasn't a bad day at all, was it? Five hours and 35

ASHTON·TATE ■

minutes of solid billable time! At your rate of $125 an hour, that's almost $700.

Step Two: Billing. After a month of such days, it's time for me to type up the bills.[3] It's a good thing we've been so methodical about remembering your time and expenses. The bills will be itemized to the minute. (The clients used to hate receiving a bill that simply stated: "For Services Rendered, $900.") A sample for one of the clients from the above mentioned daily journal is shown in Figure 2.

The statement looks a little different from those that might be prepared by any of the other professionals in this book. One necessary difference is the inclusion of expenses, which the other professionals rarely bill separately. Some attorneys may favor a less formal approach than the business-letter format I've demonstrated. The exact layout of the statement is a matter of style, of course. You might prefer to list the services and expenses together so that the dates remain in chronological order. Here, I've tried to emphasize the magnitude of the services performed by putting them first. (This idea can be carried further by isolating all the expenses on an attached page, and showing only a total in the letter.)

A final option is an aging reminder—a breakdown of the balance into the amounts current, past 30 days, past 60 days, and so on. This concept was covered in Chapter Three, but attorneys have more decisions to make. You probably want an aging reminder only on the simpler bills and on closed cases. You might also want to add a paragraph to the letter in language appropriate to the amount overdue, rather than simply giving a table.

So far, everything seems easy enough, but our example is the *simplest* kind of bill you'll ever prepare. In your profession there are several complicating factors that affect when and how you bill for your services:

> 1. One possibility is that no bill should be sent at all! The services might have been already covered by a retainer. Your agreement with the client might be to bill him only if a certain favorable result is

BILLING

ASHTON·TATE ■

LAW OFFICES
EDWIN SAMALIN

YORKTOWN OFFICE PARK
2000 MAPLE HILL STREET
P. O. BOX 427
YORKTOWN HEIGHTS, N. Y. 10598

November 1, 1983

Mr. Abe Sturms
999 Central Park West
New York, NY   10001

Re: Sturms Will

Dear Mr. Sturms:

During the past month, we provided the following services to you and incurred the following expenses on your behalf:

Date	Service	Fee
Oct. 7	Conference, 1 hour 30 minutes	$ 188.00
Oct. 10	Document preparation: will	250.00
Oct. 15	Conference, 20 minutes	42.00

Date	Expense	Amount
Oct. 10	Filing expense: will	20.00
	Total	$ 500.00

Thank you in advance for your prompt remittance.

Sincerely yours,

EDWIN SAMALIN

ESS:jbl

Figure 2. Attorney's statement of services formed and printed by the computer

achieved. If you lose the case (yes, once in a great while), perhaps you wish to bill only for expenses. In all such cases your billing system has to recognize when *not* to bill. You still want to keep track of your time and expenses, of course, for your own information.

2. Even if most of your services were covered by retainer, there might be a few "extraordinary expenses" to be billed. These should be clearly explained on the statement as unusual.

3. Perhaps the bill should be postponed. If you and your client just lost a case and you're starting the appeal process, now might not be a very good time to send a bill.

4. You might want to postpone *some* of the items. Some of your fees might be more palatable in two weeks when the outcome of a suit is known. Or they might have tax consequences for you or your client, and will be better held till January.

5. If you are the executor of an estate or the guardian of a trust fund, you might be withdrawing your fees directly from the client's funds. You should still send periodic explanations of your fees, but the statement had better not appear to be an invoice.

That's quite an array of exceptions and options, all of which have to be taken in stride by your billing system. It's problems like these that make computerization difficult, so much so that many authorities have called it impossible. Kline D. Strong, Esq., a widely acknowledged expert on law office management, once stated:

> "The preparation of a client bill which reflects effort in terms of legal services is a salient technique which every attorney should strive to master. The key to mastery of this technique is to maintain time records in such a way that the client bill may be prepared painlessly, but in detail, describing the nature of

services rendered, emphasizing the critical services and legal expertise
employed, and minimizing (but not
overlooking) ancillary services such as
numerous perfunctory telephone calls.
Such evaluation and description of legal
services cannot effectively be delegated
to a clerk nor can a computer be
programmed to make 'a silk purse out
of a sow's ear.' Billing is an *art* in the
realm of judgment and human experience, not a *science* in the realm of statistics and applied mathematics."[4]

Mr. Strong's comments *were* entirely accurate, since the accepted method of "going on computer" at the time (1970) involved giving all the firm's transaction data to an outside service bureau with a behemoth mainframe machine. Computers were simply too expensive for one law firm to own. The billing went something like the following: The firm's clerks copied the data to punched cards or (horrors!) punched tape, which meant renting bulky keypunch machines and retraining the clerks. If you didn't want to learn to punch, you could rewrite your data onto paper forms for the service bureau's own keypunch operators to convert, with a slight extra risk of errors in the conversion. After all that, in a few days you would get back your reports.

You couldn't change your mind about a transaction or correct an error without having to wait an extra day or two for the revised reports. You couldn't ask an "oddball" question on the spur of the moment ("Show me everyone who had wills prepared last year"). That is, you couldn't *interact* with the computer.

Today, the picture is entirely different. You can put a computer on your desk that is as powerful as the one the service bureaus had. The software for data management is capable enough to let you ask those "oddball" questions. (Client list management, right out of Chapter Three!) Yes, legal billing is still a difficult task and probably can't be *totally* automated even today. However, the computer can act as an assistant, showing you the bills it intends to send, but letting you have the last say. Since the computer is right there in your office for quick interaction, you can make last-minute changes.

Let the computer make the obvious decisions. Let it withhold from billing the cases known to be non-billable. Certain individual transactions will be non-billable as well (such as the "Meal-NB" entry in our sample daily journal). Let it print nice explanatory letters to the beneficiaries of the trusts. (That's not hard to do on modern computers; remember our discussion of personalized letters in Chapter Three.) In other words, let it handle the routine paperwork.

But don't forget Kline D. Strong's warning—don't expect the computer to show human judgment. Before the bills are mailed, *you* must take a look at them yourself. Feel free to cross out any items that you want not billed or delayed; add anything that comes to mind at the last minute. Then I, your secretary, can make the corrections on the spot and reprint the affected bills. You've delayed their mailing by a few hours at most.[5]

Before moving on, let me make sure I don't leave you with the misconception that Mr. Strong is old-fashioned. He has shown himself to be a true expert by embracing the new technology even though it appears to contradict some of his earlier statements. He has recently written a book to assist the smaller law office in selecting a computer.[6]

Step Three: Management Reports. At the end of the month, after all the bills have been prepared, there are several ways to extract information from our files. If the files are computerized, these reports will not require any extra work on our part. We're just harvesting our homegrown database.

You might like to see a recapitulation of the time and expenses for each case you worked on during the past

MANAGEMENT REPORTS

month. A typical "case time summary" is shown in
Figure 3.

This report doesn't shed much new light on what we've
done. It's just a condensed summary for easy reference,
and also serves as a final record of what was actually
invoiced. (To keep the example simple, I've shown only
four cases and two attorneys in your firm, Berardi and
Samalin.)

The report is arranged in alphabetical order by case
name. The last line, the Sturms case, is the simplest one;
all the work was done within one month by one attorney,
and it was all billed at a straight hourly rate. The Smith
case is slightly more involved, in that not all the work has
been billed yet for some reason not evident in the
summary.

The Spinner case is an example of the kind to be
avoided in the future. It was a contested matrimonial case
involving an acquaintance, in which a flat fee of $800 was
quoted. It turned out to require much more work than
anticipated, because the opposing lawyer insisted on going
to court. You've spent a total of 12 hours on it, but at
least it's over now. All of it has been billed, except for
the $22 lunch you picked up in relief at the case being
over for your friend and yourself.

Finally, the Stevens defense required both attorneys in
your office. It has not been billed yet because you know
that your client won't be able to pay until after she's been
proven innocent and is back at work.

A second report, a production summary, breaks down
the work by attorney rather than by case. (See Figure 4.)

Notice the ratio in the last column, the dollars billed
per billable hour. That's a "quality of case" indicator; it
will be high when most of your work is billable, and when
you're earning most of your contingent fees. We also
could have calculated dollars per total hour, obviously, but
that would confuse the issue. It might be low one month
because you've done a lot of not-immediately-pertinent
research, or you've attended a self-improvement seminar.

ASHTON·TATE ■

Case Time Summary   October 31, 1983

------------------- This Month --------------------

Case Name	Hours	Fee	Expenses	Total	Billed
Smith, John Samalin	2:45	343.75	8.50	352.25	298.25
Spinner, Ed Berardi	9:30	800.00	22.00	822.00	800.00
Stevens, June Berardi Samalin TOTAL:	 1:20 1:00 2:20	 166.67 125.00 291.67	 12.50 0.00 12.50	 179.17 125.00 304.17	 0.00 0.00 0.00
Sturms, Abe Berardi	3:40	480.00	20.00	500.00	500.00
FIRM TOTAL:	18:15	1,915.42	63.00	1,978.42	1,598.25

------------------- Year to Date -------------------

Case Name	Hours	Fee	Expenses	Total	Billed
Smith, John Samalin	8:00	1,000.00	42.00	1,042.00	988.00
Spinner, ED Berardi	12:00	800.00	22.00	822.00	800.00
Stevens, June Berardi	 1:20 1:00 2:20	 166.67 125.00 291.67	 12.50 0.00 12.50	 179.17 125.00 304.17	 0.00 0.00 0.00
Sturms, Abe Berardi	3:40	480.00	20.00	500.00	500.00
FIRM TOTAL:	26:00	2,571.67	96.50	2,668.17	2,288.00

Figure 3. Case time summary

Production Analysis -- Attorney Time Summary

	Billable Hours	Non-Billable Hours	Total Hours	Percent Billable	Amount Billed	Dollars/ Bill.Hr
C. Berardi						
Month	14:30	2:10	16:40	87	1,300.00	89.66
YTD	17:00	3:00	20:00	85	1,300.00	76.47
E. Samalin						
Month	3:45	1:00	4:45	79	298.25	79.53
YTD	9:00	2:30	11:30	78	988.00	109.78
FIRM TOTAL						
Month	18:15	3:10	21:25	85	1,598.25	87.58
YTD	26:00	5:30	31:30	83	2,288.00	88.00

Figure 4. Production analysis

There are several other ratios by which you can monitor the health of your practice. Since they depend on how many of those billable dollars are actually being received, they require additional data from your receivables department. One such ratio is the "effective billing rate," which is the actual income (billed amounts less write-offs for bad debts or unfulfilled expectations) divided by the billable hours. Some attorneys may be putting in long hours, but are not giving much attention to getting paid. They might not be billing their clients promptly, or they might simply be underselling themselves to the clients.

A third report you can get with little extra effort is a client ledger, a history of all your dealings with a particular client. Such a history can prove valuable if there is ever a dispute over the size of your bill, or over the amounts you've been withdrawing from an escrow or trust account.

Step Four: Long-Term Profitability Analysis. At this point you could be satisfied with what you've accomplished. You managed to remember every hour and every expense, and you mailed your bills promptly. You're doing better than many attorneys in avoiding the loss of money through the cracks—but avoiding loss is, in a way, still a negative accomplishment. Although you've brought your income up to 100 percent of its current potential, you haven't done anything to *increase* that potential. As long as I'm pontificating, I'll state a couple of axioms:

PROFITABILITY ANALYSIS

> *Rule of Time as a Fixed Asset*
> There are only 24 hours in the day.
> *Corollary: The Optimum Practice*
> > Given that time is a fixed resource, and given the more or less fixed market in your area, and given your natural talents, there exists one best mix of case types that optimizes your profit.

Those rules are quite true, by the way. With a little effort they could be rigorously proven. Engineers know that any time there's a fixed resource and one or more alternative ways to utilize it, there is one best way and a

ASHTON·TATE ■

corresponding maximum profit. If you can write down the following numbers—how many hours you care to work in a day, how much you earn per hour for each case type, and the maximum number of each case type you can find in your area—then there is a well-known method for finding what your maximum profit should be.

How do you get those numbers? It isn't always easy to know how much you make per hour for each case type. Our discussion so far has kept things simple by assuming a constant hourly rate for all your work. In the real world there are essentially three methods of billing for attorneys:

1. By the hour, as we've assumed so far.

2. A fixed fee. You'll often charge a flat fee for limited, short-duration services such as document preparation and filing (e.g., incorporations and wills), routine court appearances, and real estate closings. By virtue of your long experience in such matters, these may take you only a fraction of an hour. You certainly don't want to charge on a per-hour basis; you would be penalizing yourself for your experience and efficiency!

3. Contingency. When a case involves large sums of money, it often happens that a client can't pay for your work until the matter is settled. You will typically agree to work on a contingent basis. If you're successful, your fee is an agreed-upon percentage of what you've earned (or saved) for your client. If the decision is unfavorable, your fee might be nothing, just your expenses, or some minimum fee based on an hourly rate.

Especially in the third method, it can be difficult to say how much you have earned per hour. A contingency fee may be delayed for years, and then come in a fat lump sum. That is exactly the reason for keeping track of your hours—when the payment does come in, you will have some idea of how profitable the case has been.

The average earnings per hour shows up in the profitability analysis. As I explained in Chapter Three, this analysis is nothing more than a recap of every service

ASHTON·TATE ■

you've performed over a period of time, categorized and totalled by class. In Chapter Three I left the inclusion of time (profitability per hour) as an optional feature. For attorneys, it's mandatory. An example of a profitability report, as might be obtained from the routine journals you've been keeping every day, is shown in Figure 5. You'll want to be able to see that same kind of report for each attorney in the firm, and one for the entire firm.

To someone who's not an attorney, the bottom line may look pretty attractive, but we've left out a lot. We've ignored overhead: staff salaries, office rent, equipment, all the lunches and other non-billable expenses. Absolute accuracy isn't the point, however. If you want exact pictures of your profit and net worth, you can go to a fully computerized general ledger. All you care about here is the *relative* profitability of each segment of your practice. Your eyes should be drawn to the taxation line of the report—only eight percent of your time but 18.7 percent of your income. The average income per hour is the highest of them all, $161. At the other extreme are the real estate matters, which averaged only $54 an hour.

From that analysis, you can conclude that you should be concentrating more on taxation matters and less on real estate. The number of your hours that you now spend in the two areas differ by only a few percent, but what if you reversed them? What if you spent 10.9 percent of your time on taxation cases and 8.0 percent on real estate matters (assuming the hourly payoffs were the same)?

Before
On real estate:
10.9 percent x 8 hours/day = .87 hours/day average
  times $ 54.01 = $46.99 per day average
On taxation:
8.0 percent x 8 hours/day = .64 hours/day average
  times $161.29 = $103.23 per day average
Total per day from two sources = $150.22
After Switching
On real estate:
8.0 percent x 8 hours/day = .64 hours/day average

ASHTON·TATE ■

times $ 54.01 = $34.57 per day average
On taxation:
10.9 percent x 8 hours/day = .87 hours/day average
times $161.29 = $140.32 per day average
Total per day from two sources = $174.89

By reversing the hours expended on those two classes alone, you could increase your daily income from $150.22 to $174.89, a gain of $24.67 a day over the long run. That's over $6000 a year from the one improvement of a few percent! The moral of this example is that you don't have to eliminate an entire segment of your practice to see real benefits, just push a little harder in one area and relax in another.

In a firm with several attorneys, each member of the firm will have a separate section in the profitability analysis, similar to the report in Figure 5. It will make it obvious which attorneys are bringing in the bulk of the income. This is a sticky subject, and I'll voice the same warning I did at the start of the dentists' chapter: It isn't a crime for one member of the firm to bring in less than another. In fact, it's unavoidable; some work just isn't as profitable as other work. In large firms the less profitable cases and research are often assigned to the junior members. However you handle it, some sort of systematic tracking of production is required.

One final word of caution. The type of case is not always clear-cut. Your services in a single case might cover a range of types such as estate planning, tax advice, and real estate. Make your best guess at how to classify it, and don't try to interpret the profitability report over short time spans. In the long run (comparing one year to the last), the inaccuracies will average out and you'll see meaningful trends.

The Pegboard System. There is another way to streamline your manual methods without resorting to computerization. It's commonly called "pegboard accounting."

Let's review the simple manual methods we've used in our examples. You, the attorney, keep a diary of your

PEGBOARD SYSTEM

ASHTON·TATE ■

PROFITABILITY ANALYSIS

Attorney: E.S. Samalin   Period: 1-1-82 to 12-31-83

Type of Case	Hours Spent	% of Total Hours	Dollars Earned	% of Total Dollars	$/Hour
Billable					
Commercial	68	3.5	7,480	5.6	110.00
Cont. Matr.	200	10.3	16,750	12.5	83.75
Criminal	292	15.0	18,100	13.5	61.99
Estate	186	9.5	18,970	14.2	101.99
Negligence	123	6.3	11,685	8.7	95.00
Real Estate	212	10.9	11,450	8.5	54.01
Taxation	155	8.0	25,522	18.7	161.29
Uncont.Matr.	250	12.8	24,522	18.3	98.09
Total Billable	1486	76.2	133,957	100.0	90.15
Unbillable					
Administ.	155	8.0			
Education	90	4.6			
Personal	64	3.4			
Research	154	7.9			
Total Unbillable	463	23.8			
Attorney Total	1949	100.0	133,957	100.0	68.73

Figure 5. Profitability analysis

time and expenses. The diary might not be recognizable as such if it's scattered over dozens of paper scraps, but it's technically a diary. I, your secretary, recopy those entries into a single daily journal (sometimes called a "recap sheet"). I copy the same entries several more times to get the billing statement, the profitability analysis, and the client ledger.

The problem is obvious—too much copying. That's the inefficiency attacked by a pegboard system. In our first step, entering time and expenses into the daily journal, we don't use ordinary paper. We write them by hand onto a time slip, which carries its own small strip of carbon paper on the back side of the one-line entry. The time slip is placed on top of the recap sheet, so that the one entry creates records in both places. The correct alignment of the two sheets is assured by placing them both on a board with a vertical row of pegs on the left side. The pegs match holes in the time slip and recap sheet.

The charges still have to be recopied to get the bill, but the billing form has several carbon copies. The original goes to the client. One copy, with the time slips attached, satisfies our need for a client ledger.

The pegboard system is a good start. It forces you to be organized and complete in your timekeeping, and it reduces the number of manual copying operations to one or two. In fact, when computers were slower and more expensive than they are now, the pegboard system was the *best* data management system available.

WHERE CAN A COMPUTER HELP?

After all that background, it's clear (to me anyway) that the computer can't run the entire show. You can't dump all your scraps of paper onto the keyboard and expect the money to roll in. But a good data *management* system, made up of a computer and a good human assistant, can be well worth the investment. The computer's role is to organize the records, speed up statement processing, monitor your receivables, and eliminate manual copying. The assistant's job is to make you and the computer understand each other.

ASHTON·TATE ■

First, you must determine the kinds of information you need to remember—or as explained in Chapter Two, determining the fields in the database. In this example I'll keep both the services and expenses in one file, the same way they were entered in the paper daily journal.

Structure of Transaction Database
Client name
Name of case
Attorney name or identifier (if more than one in the firm)
Class of case (negligence, estate, criminal, etc.)
Billing type
Type of service or expense
Time spent
Date
Amount
Billed yet? (A yes-or-no field, to prevent billing an item twice)
Postponement date (for services you want to hold for later billing)
Comment

A couple of items need clarification. The "billing type" specifies how the amount is to be billed: at a straight hourly rate, as a fixed fee, on a contingent basis, or as an expense (remember that both services and expenses are contained in this file). We might use a single letter to identify the billing type: H, F, C, or E.

The "type of service or expense" identifies what was actually performed or incurred. Typical contents might be Conference, Trial, or Document Preparation; Tolls or Telephone; Filing Fees. We need to decide at the outset upon some standard abbreviations for all these types, to save time and avoid misspellings. Usually a programmer will resort to numerical codes. I've seen the following choices from one service bureau:

Service Codes	Expense Codes
01 Conference with Client	01 Filing Fee
20 Attendance at Court	02 Recording Fee
37 Letter to Title Company	12 Tolls
79 Prepare Trial Brief	20 Title Insurance

There's no rule that numbers have to be used; the computer really doesn't care one way or the other. But given the wide range of possible services, numbers are usually easier to make up and remember than literal abbreviations. The difference will be felt only by your assistant, the person who enters the data. On all your reports and on the clients' statements, the codes can easily be reconverted back to full descriptions.

Going further, we could substitute codes for the "class of case" as well. The same service bureau uses all of the following:

17 Formation of business
18 Maintenance of business
19 Sale or merger of business
20 Acquisition of business
21 Dissolution of business

It is debatable, however, whether such detail is worthwhile. As I warned before, the type-of-case data will only be informative over the long run anyway. It would be better to view the type-of-case data as a generic classification and use, in this example, simply Businesses. (Even if your profitability analysis tells you that formation of a business is profitable and selling it isn't, are you really going to tell the owner of a business to find another lawyer in midstream?)

We'll need other files to remember historical information: (1) A case history file to accumulate the hours and dollars associated with each case; (2) an attorney history file for the same purpose, but for each member of the firm; (3) a class history file for the totals in each general class of work. We'll also need the ever-present client list—a file of names, addresses, phone numbers, and so on for each client. That's where we'll get the mailing address for the statements, for example; there's no need to duplicate the address in each and every transaction.

Now we're ready to outline (in structured English, remember) the procedure for timekeeping and billing. It's a somewhat different outline in that it spells out when the computer works and when the humans do. That's the result of our conclusion that two of the steps—review of the daily time records and preview of the statements—need human judgment. (Actually, three of the steps need human judgment. I'm willing to bet that computers will never be able to read a client's name from a smudged and wrinkled paper napkin!)

Legal Timekeeping and Billing Procedure
Timekeeping:

Assistant: Enter time and expense records as best you can.

Computer: Print all the entries in a readable report:
all entries for a single case together,
all entries for a single day together, if more than one day has been entered.
Point out any obvious omissions, including:
Expenses incurred but no time
Critical fields missing (client name)
Client or case name unheard of (probable misspelling)
Amount more than $1,000 (are you serious or is it a typo?)
More than ten hours billed in one day
No entries for known appointments (if your computer also knows your appointments, as we'll discuss later)

Attorney: Review and pencil in corrections.
Assistant: Enter corrections.

Billing (end of month, or individual bills on demand):

Computer: Print billing preview reports on a high speed printer:

ASHTON·TATE ■

For each attorney,
   For each case,
      List all billable items (those not post-poned, not contingent, and not specifically marked as non-billable. When in doubt assume billable.)
      In date order.
      If more than one attorney worked on the case, show *all* fees on the principal attorney's preview.
      Add the billable amounts to show the invoice amount.
      Show the aging reminder if there are past-due amounts.[7]

Attorneys: Review the billing report. Cross out items not billable or to be postponed. (Those are probably the only two corrections at this point; mark them "N" or "P" for expediency.)

Assistant: Enter the corrections. (Requires only a few keystrokes per correction, changing billing type or postponement date.)

Computer: Print the final statements on letterhead and envelopes.
Enter "Yes" in the Billed-Yet? field.
Add the new current balances into the receivables file.
Add the total amounts and hours into the case and attorney historical files.
Add the total amounts and hours for each case class into the class history file.

Reporting (all optional and all by the computer):
Case Time Summary
   For each case,
      For each attorney,
         Print the month's:
            total hours billable,
            the fee,
            expenses,

total billable (fee + expenses),
total billed.
Show the same figures for year-to-date (consult the case history file)
Add all the columns to show the case totals.
Add all the case totals to show a firm total.

Production Analysis (Attorney Time Summary):
For each attorney:
Print the month's:
total billable hours,
total non-billable hours,
total hours (add the first two),
percentage billable,
amount billed,
ratio of amount billed to billable hours.
Do the same for year-to-date (consult the attorney history file).
Add all the hours and dollar columns to get the firm's total.
Print the firm's percentage billable and amount per billable hour.

Profitability Analysis:
For each attorney:
Using the class history file:
For each billable case class:
Print:
total hours for the class,
percentage of those hours over the total billable hours,
total amount for the class,
percentage of that amount over the total billable amount,
ratio of amount to total hours.
Add the hours and amounts to get the total billables.
Print the percentage of the total billable hours over all hours.
Print the average dollars/hour for all billables.
For each non-billable class:

Print:

> total hours,
>
> percentage of those hours over the total non-billable,

Add the hours to get the total non-billable hours.
Print the percentage of non-billable hours over all hours.

Print the total hours, total amount, and dollars/hour for the attorney.

Print the attorney's percentage of hours and amount in relation to the entire firm.

Print the firm's total hours and amounts.

That's the procedure, but it's only a skeleton. You might ask for any number of other reports, such as a full receivables or a delinquents report to check up on your collection performance. A client ledger might be needed at any time. You'll think of new questions to ask as you go along. I can think of a couple more just from going through that procedure:

> A list of all the postponed billable amounts, to make sure you don't forget a few. (This bears a kinship with the open item report of Chapter Three.)
>
> An analysis of uncollected bills broken down by class of case. Maybe one of the classes that appears to be lucrative on the profitability analysis has a high incidence of unpaid bills.

This demonstrates two of the major reasons for drawing up an outline, be it for a computerized or a manual procedure—it generates ideas, and makes you see where the loopholes are.

CALENDAR CONTROL

Finally, we come to the second major application for a data manager in a legal office. It will be a lot easier to analyze because there aren't nearly as many special cases and exceptions as there were in timekeeping and billing.

The calendar is a stern, unforgiving taskmaster to an attorney. A large number of deadlines are critical, in the sense that if you miss them, your client's affairs take a

ASHTON·TATE ■

noticeable turn for the worse. (Your chances of being paid take at least as sharp a nosedive.) Examples of this group are the dates of a court appearance, a bankruptcy hearing, a meeting of creditors, a deadline for filing objections, scheduled depositions, deadlines for filing briefs, pretrial conferences, expiration of statutes of limitation, and patent or trademark renewal dates in foreign countries.

Slightly less critical dates are administrative meetings, regular appointments with clients, scheduled periodic reviews of files, and deadlines for completion of research projects.

Last and least is a group of excusable misses: anniversaries, birthdays, the first day of work for a new employee, seminars, conferences, and personal appointments (dental, medical, tonsorial, or tee-off).

Keeping track of all these dates is an ideal job for a computer. You can design the database just by thinking of the notes you write on your own calendar:

Date
Time (if any)
Place
Description of the event
Name of the related case, if any

An optional field is the attorney's name, if several attorneys are sharing the same system. Another is the class of event, such as administrative, personal, or trial. That's to allow you later on to ask for a listing of all the deadlines in a particular class, such as all the trademark expiration dates in the next three months. Maybe you're in the mood for working on trademarks this week!

You or your assistant can simply enter each deadline as you become aware of it. On Monday morning the computer can quickly give you a list of all the important dates coming up during the week or month, nicely printed on pocket-sized paper. The procedure is simple with a good data manager: "Show me all events for which the Date falls between today and a month from today."

Now I don't pretend that this one application will justify the cost of a computer. An assistant with a large calendar

and a typewriter could do the same thing for you. But if you already have a computer this will save some time, especially if there are several attorneys in the firm who need typed reminders. There are additional benefits:

- You can be automatically reminded to set dates for regular weekly or monthly meetings, in time to notify all concerned. For that, add another field to the database—Frequency—which can be weekly, monthly, yearly, or nothing. Then the inquiry is, "Show me all events with a monthly Frequency which haven't had a new Date set yet." Or, "Show me all events with a yearly Frequency which *should* come up in the next 60 days."
- Knowing your appointments lets the computer do a better job of checking your timekeeping entries. (See the timekeeping outline in the last section.)
- If you wish to go the limit, you can let the computer schedule your appointments. I personally am not too enthusiastic about computerized schedulers (as evidenced by my remarks in the dentists' chapter), but this can be helpful for arranging meetings between several persons in a large firm.

LITIGATION SUPPORT

As briefly described at the beginning of this chapter, a litigation support system is designed to quickly find key words, names, or references out of the mass of thousands of documents sometimes associated with complex cases. It can be an essential aid in the large corporate and government cases. But those cases where the benefit is obvious aren't the ones that fit well on small computers.

To get a feel for the magnitude of the problem, imagine that there are 10,000 documents involved, a number not at all unusual in such matters. Let's assume that we don't wish to remember *complete* documents, except maybe in a few critical instances such as briefs and depositions. We only want an abstract of less than 1000 characters (less than half a page). Somewhere, we have to store 10,000 times 1000 characters. A total of ten million characters! That's either at the limit or beyond the limit of the average small computer today. It can be done (it's possible to add storage devices capable of up to 100 million characters), but it will be slow. I estimate that an exhaustive search through 10 million characters will take on the order of ten minutes to an hour on a good micro-computer.[8]

Litigation support systems are normally handled by large (million dollar class) machines owned by companies that make this their business. When you ask a question like, "How many of the documents in the 10,000 contain the key word 'pollution'?", you don't mind waiting between one and ten seconds on the best systems. It's fast enough so that you can ask questions of only casual interest, and do a little unstructured research.

Another reason for letting an outside firm run the system is the cost of entering all that data. Someone has to devote the time to reading 10,000 documents and then have the skill to abstract it. On top of that, 10,000 abstracts of 1,000 characters each is going to require about 600 hours of fast, accurate typing just for the entry!

However, if you only have to keep an eye on a mere 1,000 or so documents, and if you can bring your require-ments down to short abstracts and key items like name, date, and title, you should consider doing it yourself. The size of the whole file will be less than a million charac-ters, and simple searches will take a minute or two. Searches through a limited number of key words will take ten to 20 seconds. The time for manually entering the data is reasonable, perhaps one solid week of a paralegal assistant's time.

Once you've selected a good, fast computer and a good, fast data management software package, and you've entered all the text you need, the actual usage is relatively simple. Our explanation of client list management in Chapter Three covered the fundamentals. You'll be able to ask questions like:

> "Show me the titles of all documents written by John Doe between January and April, 1980."

ASHTON·TATE ■

"Show me all the titles that concern pollution, which have not yet been produced to the opposing counsel."

If you have cases that produce this many documents, and you've found yourself missing important references (or complaining about the number of people you've had to hire *not* to miss them), then go right ahead and invest in your own computer. A litigation support system of this size is quite practical on a small computer (less than $10,000) without the programming costing you more than the computer itself.

SUMMARY

Timekeeping and time-related billing are the unique problems of attorneys that have made data management systems slow in coming to the legal office, despite the fact that many offices already have word processing computers. The delay is not due to lack of equipment. One aggravating factor has been the resistance of many attorneys to following any systematic method for recording time and expenses. Another is the fact that the billing procedure isn't cut and dried. There are enough exceptions and choices so that the attorney still has to exercise personal judgment over the statements.

These problems have led some analysts to predict that computerized billing won't be practical until the attorney has his or her own computer and learns to use it. That would certainly help, but I don't think it's really necessary. The methods I've outlined in this chapter do not require the attorney to use the computer, although *someone* in the office has to. The methods take advantage of the ease of making trial runs and last-minute corrections on a computer of your own, a capability you do not have when you're renting time on someone else's machine. The computer becomes just one partner in a data management *system*. It handles the routine work, and steps aside to let humans exercise the necessary judgment. The two critical steps are the correction of time records as soon as possible, and the preview of statements before they're sent.

ASHTON·TATE ■

Notes

1. From the article "Selling the Legal Marketplace" by James C. Dunlap, in *Computer Dealer* magazine, February 1983, pp. 56-62.

2. What if you have clients (probably corporate) large enough to be involved in more than one case at a time? It would be possible, of course, to add another column to the time sheet specifying the name of the case. That's often called the 'Matter" column. Another solution is to make up different client names for each case, as if each one were a different person. 'Smith Will" or "Smith Closing" or "Smith Suit."

3. As a tactical matter, you shouldn't wait until the month's end to send all your bills. If a case has come to a clearly recognizable end, bill *now*! Don't wait until the client's gratitude (or acceptance of fate, as the case may be) wears off.

4. From the 1970 article "The Sans-Copy System for Obtaining Financial and Management Data sans Computers," reprinted in the 1979 collection *Practicing Law Profitably* by Kline D. Strong, 1039 Vista View Drive, Salt Lake City, Utah 84108.

5. Better yet, don't make the changes directly on the final bills. Have the computer give you a condensed list of all the time and expenses it intends to send. You might call that a "billing preview report." Since this is for correction purposes only, it can be printed on a high-speed printer (one which gives a less than perfect appearance) to save time. The final bills will be prepared on a letter-quality printer (which means slower), so they should be done only once.

6. *Choosing and Using Computers* by Kline D. Strong, published by the American Bar Association, 1155 E. 60th St., Chicago, Ill. 60637.

7. The aging is determined according to the procedure outlined in Chapter Three, a simple moving of balances from one past-due drawer to the next. Finance charges can also be calculated at this point if desired. Notice that even though this preview report is by nature a trial run, the aging can be performed and permanently recorded. An attorney's corrections will affect only the current balance.

8. That pessimistic time was for an exhaustive search, to find all the occurrences of an arbitrary word. If you limit your searching power to only a small number (say ten) *key* words in each document, the picture is better. You can build separate files of just the key words and search through them in under a minute.

ASHTON·TATE ■

Chapter 7

Pharmacists

Pharmacists share many data management needs with doctors and dentists. This is hardly surprising since a pharmacist is a health-care professional too. But a pharmacy is also a retail store, which creates a whole new set of problems. If you are a pharmacist, some of your income is derived from fees for services (as is the case for dentists and doctors), but a large part of it comes from profits on sales. You're forced to be a businessperson to a greater extent than the other professionals because you have to worry about sales volume, cost of goods sold, inventory turnover, and all the other concerns of a retailer.

This chapter will begin with a look at the needs you share with other professionals: forms handling, accounts receivable control, profitability analysis, and client list management. Then, we'll look more deeply into your special requirements: inventory control and the monitoring of adverse drug interactions.

Forms handling is a significant advantage of computerization in a pharmacy. Paperwork abounds: the prescription that starts the transaction, the bottle label, the receipt, perhaps a mailing label, and a possible bill to a third party. We have already established in this book that a

PAPERWORK

ASHTON·TATE ■

computer can print all these forms faster than you can type them manually. If the customer, as is usually the case, is one who has received a prescription from you before, then the name and address are already known to the computer. You will have to identify the person *somehow* to the computer, of course (computers that recognize faces aren't a commodity yet), but typically you will only have to type a six-digit identifying number, or on the easier-to-use systems, the first few letters of the last name. Even if there's more than one person with that same last name, you'll have to type at most another digit or two to select from the much smaller set.

In either case, let's say you have to enter six characters of some kind to specify the person. Even after identifying the doctor, the name of the drug, and the instructions, with a computer you will have entered about 40 keystrokes—less than you used to type manually just for the bottle label. The rest is automatic: a sequential prescription number, the standard warnings for the drug ("may cause drowsiness"), the date, the price, a third-party bill, and an updating of the patient's record.

This benefit alone—the reduction of manual paper-work—can justify the investment in a computer system. One pharmacist, for example, reported that a single professional could fill well over 100 prescriptions in a regular (no overtime) day.[1] Each prescription required less than 90 seconds of attendance at the computer. Before the computer was installed, each prescription had required about five minutes, or over eight hours of paperwork for the 100 prescriptions! He was able to reduce his staff by one pharmacist; that paid for the computer system in under a year. In addition, everyone could go home when the doors closed, without a briefcase full of forms to fill out after dinner.

One of the necessary ingredients for this reduction of manual labor, in any computer system, is the conversion of a standard set of names and descriptions to a standard set of codes. The codes are usually, but not necessarily, numerical. In this case, the drug names are standardized by National Drug Code numbers (NDC). These numbers include three component pieces of information, as in this example:

```
00081-0019-82
     │    │    └── The size of the package
     │    └── The product itself
     └── The manufacturer of the drug
```

The fact that an accepted national coding system is already available is a great boost for computerization. This one is especially helpful because it includes, in a convenient condensed form, a complete description of each product. The designer of your data management system doesn't have to create a numbering scheme and teach you to use it. The system can continue to use the same codes you and your suppliers are familiar with.

Other codes, not so conveniently standardized, are frequently used in pharmaceutical data management. The instructions on the prescription label are often coded since they're somewhat lengthy and many of them are used repeatedly. Thus, you might choose the number "12" to represent "Take two every four hours." These are called SIG codes, from the word "SIG" on the doctor's prescription (the Latin "signa" means instructions). Additional codes may be used, as desired, for other wordy descriptions like warnings, doctor names, and pharmacist names.

You can see that the computer is replacing a lot of paper-and-pencil pushing with a small number of keystrokes. If you're a two-finger typist like me, you'd like to go even further and do away with the keystrokes as well. The computer cannot understand your spoken words (not yet, anyway), but a few of your chores can already be performed by one computer reading the data directly from another with little human intervention. In Chapter Four (Physicians) we discussed the possibility of transmitting insurance claims over the phone (ECS); that might be practical for you now, depending upon how much third-party billing you do, what kind, and what area of the country you're in. A more widespread application of elec-

ASHTON·TATE ■

tronic data transfer is the placing of orders to drug wholesalers; we'll return to this in the last section on inventory
control.

The alternative method of exchanging data in "machine-
readable form," usually a magnetic disk sent through the
mail, is already being used in pharmacies for a periodic
update of the standard drug price list. Drug pricing
services, or the manufacturers themselves, will provide a
magnetic disk containing, in a form your computer can
read, each drug's name, NDC number, and its various
prices (direct, AWP, welfare, and any others relating to
local regulations).

PRICING

Pricing can be extremely complicated. The wide range
of prices a pharmacy must offer is a headache shared by
few other retail stores or other professionals. I've
mentioned two variables in the prices the pharmacy itself
pays: direct price and AWP. The direct price is the cost
of a drug if it is ordered directly from the manufacturer.
Whether or not you are entitled to order in this way
depends on the manufacturer and your volume. The alternative is to order through a wholesaler, which, of course,
costs you a little more. That's the AWP, Average Wholesale Price.

But the real complexity occurs in the prices to the
public. Some of the variations are mandatory, encompas-
sing welfare or third-party plans provided by employers,
unions, or governments. Others you might institute yourself as marketing aids, to attract customers by offering a
special rate: senior citizens, schools, nursing homes,
doctors, or even your own employees. Some pharmaceutical systems will allow even more detailed breakdowns in
prices according to the quantity purchased, the type of
drug, or the type of purchase (walk-in cash, phone order,
credit, and so on). You can end up with a system containing hundreds of different formulas involving several variables, a system you could never maintain manually.

Typically these variations are defined by *tables* which
specify your fee as a function of the cost of the drug. An

Name of Plan or Rate	Ranges of Drug Costs Fees (fixed amount or percentage)				
Sr. Citizens Rate	10.00 1.00	20.00 1.50	30.00 2.00	40.00 2.50	70.00 3.00
Plan 1: Teacher's Union	10.00 2.50	15.00 2.75	20.00 3.00	40.00 3.20	50.00 3.50
Plan 2: Blue Cross	10.00 1.00	20.00 2.00	50.00 3.00	90.00 4.00	
Plan 3: Blue Cross	10.00 11.00%	20.00 10.00%	50.00 9.00%	100.00 8.00%	
Plan 3: Medicaid	10.00 2.60	20.00 2.60	30.00 2.60	40.00 2.60	50.00 2.60

Figure 1. Pharmacist's fee schedule

example of a pricing table is shown in Figure 1. For each plan, the top row shows the ranges in standard costs, while the bottom one shows the corresponding markup as either a fixed fee or a percentage multiplier.

The widespread use of third-party plans has a strong impact on the value of your *accounts receivable*. In many pharmacies such plans are the *only* receivables. Allowing customers to buy on credit is not nearly as common a practice as it used to be. Even for customers who don't belong to a plan, bank credit cards—Master Card, Visa and the like—are usually a better approach to credit buying. Then the receivable is the bank's paperwork, not yours. The same "no unnecessary receivables" attitude generally extends to insurance claims as well. Let the customer pay you and submit the claim on his own.

Thus, third-party plans represent by far the largest chunk, if not all, of your receivables. The nightmare here is at least as bad as the one I analyzed in the physicians' chapter. You pharamacists have a greater number of smaller plans to keep track of; it appears that every local government, union, and large company has a different plan. You also operate with a much smaller margin of profit, so you're less able to tolerate the errors and delays.

Fortunately, most of the plans do agree on a standard form for the submission of claims. The universal drug claim form looks very much like the charge slip used by the bank cards. Individual plans do, however, vary in the particular information to be entered on the form. Some might require a social security number, or the buyer's age, or a second means of identification. Thus, a good feature to look for in a computerized data manager is a way to allow for these exceptions—a way you can add or change the information to be printed on the universal claim form.

Pharmacists have the same frustrating problems as physicians with Medicaid: rejected claims (one paramcist estimated a 25 percent rejection rate), garbled codes, and underpaid fees. A typical case involved a drug with a standard cost of $11 and an allowed fee of $2.60, for which

Medicaid remitted $3.50. (If they had paid $3.60, I might believe they'd dropped a digit!) Even when the system works well it's not very profitable (at least in New York State); the pharmacy is allowed to charge only a flat fee of $2.60, no matter how much the drug costs. This explains that strange-looking bottom row in the pricing table. Unfortunately, I don't think a computer can help much here, even with the *third-party tracking* method we outlined in Chapter Four. There isn't enough margin to justify the inquiry letters and phone calls you would have to make after the computer brought the errors to your attention.

Profitability analysis is a natural by-product of a pharmacy's homegrown database, just as it is for the other professionals. However, the information contained in the analysis is different. Unlike doctors and dentists, the pharmacist's services do not fall into clearly defined procedure codes. Unlike lawyers, pharmacists do not concentrate much on the time value of their services. The important statistics are:

- •The split between drug costs and the pharmacist's fees (which together add up to the total income for prescriptions).
- •The percentage of new prescriptions versus refills.
- •The percentage of third-party payments versus private payments.
- •Within the class of private payments, the breakdown among cash, charge, and (optionally) credit card.
- •Within the class of third-party payments, the percentage due to each of the possible plans and the average fee.

Client list management, even in its simplest forms, can be highly beneficial in a pharmacy. The clearest example is just a list of all your past customers. This list, especially when it is generated by a computer which can take over the work of typing letters and mailing labels, will allow

ASHTON·TATE ■

you to make an effective direct mail announcement of a new pharmacist joining your store, or even the opening of a new store. For the new store announcement, though, you will probably want to be a little more selective. You can minimize your mailing costs while still reaching the customers who will be most interested, by notifying only those who live closer to the new location than to your current one. Zip codes are an easy way to make that distinction. The request you would ask your data manager—following the standard form presented in Chapter Two—might be, "Show me all customers for whom the zip code is 10589, 10590, or 10598."

Another very simple application for a data management system is the retrieval of prescriptions by name of the customer. Often, one of your clients (usually a long-time client) will walk in and say something like, "You filled a prescription for me a few months ago, and I'd like a refill..." If you are in a typical busy pharmacy, with your prescription file organized by number, you might be tempted to tell the customer to come back the next day, to give yourself time to find the name in the file. But if your files are managed by a computer, the last name is as good a way as any to look for a record. In a few seconds you'll have the prescription, along with the rest of that client's history if you want it.

This is the most important benefit of client list management in a pharmacy—the easy retrieval of a customer's history, including all the drugs that have been prescribed in the past, the doctors, and the diagnoses. Maintaining this "patient profile" is mandated by law in some states. Certainly you can maintain such a file manually. There are standard filing systems available, or you could do it with nothing more than a looseleaf binder with one sheet devoted to each customer, in alphabetical order. During your spare moments, or every night after you've closed your doors, all you have to do is copy to the appropriate page all the following information from each prescription filled during the day:

Drug
Dosage
Date
Doctor
Diagnosis
Renewal instructions, if any

If it takes you one minute to copy all that data to the profiles, and you fill 100 prescriptions per day, you will only lose a couple of hours of your spare time every night.

But if you're already entering all of those fields into a computerized database, there's no more work to do. Even if there is some copying to be done, say from a daily transactions file to a history file, it will certainly proceed a lot faster than you can do it by hand. This is exactly what we meant by a homegrown database in Chapter Two. With no extra effort you have gained a resource, an asset that will pay dividends whenever you want to ask questions like:

"Show me everyone who should have a prescription refilled in the next few days." This allows you to provide a reminder service much like the patient recall described in the dentists' chapter.

"Show me everyone over the age of 40 who has taken Yaphrax in the last two years." You just received a warning letter from the manufacturer.

"Show me everyone who was prescribed the drug Googol more than six months ago." You just found out that it has a decidely limited shelf life, and should be discarded if any is still sitting in the medicine cabinet.

I've purposely picked three inquiries that are global in nature—you want to sift through *all* of your past customers. But what about inquiries into a specific *single* customer's history, the kind you might want to ask when the person walks through your door? Our search-by-name problem is a good example: "What prescription did Mary Smith fill three months ago?". It could be handled by manual methods, like the looseleaf binder system described above. But even here it's possible for the volume of information to get out of hand. If you start asking questions about interactions with a wide range of drugs ("Does this drug prescribed for Mary Smith have adverse side effects with any other drug she might be taking?"), the question becomes global again, involving a universe of possible interactions. This brings us to our first pharmacy-specific application.

MONITORING DRUG INTERACTIONS

There are two basic motivations for having a computer check for adverse side effects when filling a prescription: to protect the patient, and to create customer loyalty. Consider the following story:[2]

> Last spring, a customer entered a drugstore near Syracuse, N.Y., with a prescription for the drug Cyclapen. The drug could have seriously hurt her. The woman was allergic to a Cyclapen ingredient, penicillin. Her new doctor didn't know that. But the pharmacist, by checking his new patient-records computer, found out. After consulting with her doctor, he substituted a penicillin-free drug.
>
> "She was ecstatic that he caught it in time," recalls the pharmacist. "If she'd taken it, she would have been in shock by the time she was in the parking lot. Now, she's a regular here."

The first motivation, to protect the patient, is certainly a worthy one, but it raises several disturbing questions of responsibility and liability. If in five years, as is predicted,[3] more than half the pharmacies indeed have such computer systems, are you guilty of malpractice if you don't have one? For that matter, if you do have one but it isn't the latest and best system, are you liable? I can imagine the expert witness for the prosecution saying, "In my professional judgment, the best systems of this type would have caught the interaction that made Mrs. Smith ill." No doubt the doctor who prescribed the drug will be in the courtroom with you, but that's small comfort.

In the future, someone—preferably an official body like the American Medical Association—will no doubt publish an official database of drug interactions. Every pharmacy

ASHTON·TATE ■

in the country will be able to use the standardized information, and avoid legal questions like these.

What would such a database look like? It would contain two kinds of interactions: drug-drug and drug-allergy. Undoubtedly the drugs would be classified by some unique coding system, like the current NDC codes. A coding system will also be needed for allergies, such as the one already formulated by the ASHP (American Society of Hospital Pharmacists). In order to keep things simple, which is always desirable in a standard, there might even be two separate databases for the two types of interactions, with the following fields:

Drug Interaction Database:
    Drug Code
    Interacting Drug Code
Allergy Interaction Database:
    Drug Code
    Interacting Allergy Code

To get these simple two-field structures, I've assumed that there will be one record for every possible interaction. (If any of these terms are unfamiliar to you, refer to Chapter Two.) A drug with ten different possible reactions would have ten records. Each of those records would contain just two numbers:

    Drug Code: 00002035102
    Interacting: 00005321434

Then, the method the computer would have to follow whenever you are about to dispense a drug, is:

Drug Interactions Procedure:
Given the NDC code of the drug to be dispensed (the drug name has already been looked up and verified by the druggist):
Find that Drug Code in the Drug Interactions Database.
If there are any interactions listed,
  For each such interaction:
    Compare the Interacting Drug Code with all the ones in the patient's history file.
    If there is a match,

> Warn the user: flash the name of the possible interacting drug on the screen, sound a bell. Continue for all interactions listed for the drug to be dispensed. (There might be more than one!)
>
> If there are no interactions (or no matching ones), verify that negative finding (but without the bell).

The same outline, with a few words changed, could be applied equally well to the allergy database. Notice that the computer is told to show *some* kind of result even if it is negative. That's to avoid the possibility, remote though it may be, that you are about to prescribe some drug that was accidentally omitted from the official database. Even a drug that is absolutely safe, that has no known interactions, should be included in the database, along with some code that means no interaction (maybe all zeroes?) as a double precaution against this kind of error.[4]

INVENTORY CONTROL

A large retail store like a supermarket, which derives its profit solely from the conversion of inventory into sales, needs a comprehensive method of inventory control. Let's look at this complete method first, but reserve judgment on whether a pharmacy needs all the features.

If you are responsible for controlling the inventory of a supermarket, you have two basic objectives:

1. Never run out of goods the public wants to buy.
2. Never have too many of them on hand.

It's the second objective that is difficult. If you only wanted to satisfy the first one, you could simply stock large numbers of everything. But that wastes floor space, ties up your cash, and leaves you with products you cannot sell (either through spoilage or loss of favor in the public eye). At the other extreme, if you're too stingy with your stock, you will frequently run out of items when you could have sold them. That means an immediate lost sale as well as a longer-range loss of customers, once they get the feeling that your store "never" has what they want.

ASHTON·TATE ■

And the items will continue to be out of stock for as long as it takes the vendor to ship your next order.

The sensible compromise is to stock the minimum amount that will satisfy the public's needs, for the length of time it takes to receive a new shipment from the vendor. Well, not quite. Let's say you've determined that it takes two weeks to receive an order of aspirin, and that the public will buy about 100 bottles in two weeks. If you order only 100 bottles at a time, you will be placing an order every two weeks! That's a lot of paperwork for you and the vendor. The paperwork on the vendor's side will be reflected in a higher cost to you, higher than it would be if you ordered 1000 bottles at a time. You can save money by ordering in larger quantities, but the savings has to be balanced against the costs of storage.

Thus, your real objective is to stock the minimum amount of each item that ensures you will never be out of an item the public wants, *and* that your overall costs—the total for the purchase, storage, and paperwork—are minimized.[5] The amount that satisfies that objective is known as the "economic order quantity" (EOQ). Obviously, it's a different number for each item in your inventory, since it depends on the vendor's pricing, shelf life, cost of storage, and lead time for ordering.

If you are using purely manual methods of inventory control in your hypothetical supermarket, you probably don't know exactly how much stock you have on hand at any given time. You probably would use a *periodic* method of inventory control. You physically count your stock once per period (weekly, monthly, or longer). You count each and every can and bottle. As the days pass after your last count, you become less and less sure of how many you have. In this periodic system, the economic order quantity (EOQ) is a very approximate number, rooted in your experience and skill at estimating the public's desires. You're not likely to change it often, once you have found a number that works reasonably well over the long run. So, you might place an order for 20 hairbrushes every month, even though that leaves you with a slight excess at

some times and an occasional outage at others. Only if an obvious overage problem develops—hairbrushes spilling into the aisle, for example—are you likely to adjust the order quantity before the date of your next count.

A computerized inventory system, on the other hand, can easily handle the boring job of subtracting each and every sale of an item from your stock total. That's known as the *perpetual* method of inventory control. The computer can, in theory, tell you exactly how many of each item you have at any moment.[6] True perpetual inventory control, however, is a lot of work even with a computer. You have to tell the system about every shipment of goods that comes in, and every significant loss of product to spoilage. You might as well go all the way and let the computer help with your purchasing, accounts payable, and general ledger.[7] Furthermore, to make this approach really practical, you have to let the computer know about each sale *as it occurs*; otherwise you'll have to type all your daily receipts into the computer each night. That means one of three things:

  1. You need a cash register that is "smart" enough to send all the sales information to a computer. That's the most likely solution for a large retailer like a supermarket. Multiple registers store the sales data during the day, and then transmit the numbers to a large computer in the back room at night.
  2. The computer *is* the cash register. This is sufficient for a small retailer with only one sales counter. A personal computer can be combined with a cash drawer to act like a very smart cash register.
  3. A computer is installed just for the purpose of controlling inventory. Each sale is entered into the computer, *then* rung up again on a cash register.

The third approach may seem wasteful, and is for a straight retail store, but a pharmacy has enough other reasons for using a computer so that this method is often the right solution. A cash register would not be capable of printing labels for bottles, or looking out for adverse drug interactions, for example. So, the prescription is filled with the aid of the computer, but the actual exchange of money is still done at the register in the same way that everything else is sold. A pharmacy seldom needs to monitor all the non-prescription items (hairbrushes, razors, etc.) on the computer.

For all these reasons—a pharmacy is not just a retail store, all items don't need to be tracked, and there are other good uses for a computer—a less comprehensive inventory system is usually preferable in a pharmacy. There are three easier methods.

Perpetual Inventory of Prescription Drugs Only. The computer already knows how many units of each prescription drug you've sold. Therefore, for this subset of your overall stock, you get perpetual inventory control with little extra effort. You do have to tell the computer about new orders, when they arrive, and wastage; but you'll probably want to keep track of those numbers anyway (especially for controlled substances and perishables). One extra chore that has to be performed at the outset is to tell the computer the economic order quantity for each drug. As discussed above, that's an estimate you make from the drug cost, shelf life, lead time, and the available quantity discounts. In return, you'll get a "want list" of drugs to be reordered, complete with recommended order quantities. And, assuming the computer is keeping the drug prices and the vendor addresses, it's a simple matter to let the computer print the orders.[8]

Complete Inventory Utilization Report. This approach and the next one are essentially manual methods. You do not enter inventory levels or the economic order quantities into the computer. It doesn't attempt to track what is on hand or how much to order. *You* place the orders. The computer does know, however, the quantities of prescription drugs you have dispensed. It assists your ordering with a "Complete Inventory Utilization" report, which might look like this:

Drug Name	NDC Number	Dispensed This Month	Dispensed Last Month
Darvocet-N 50 Tablet	00002035102	500	450
Darvon-N 100MG Tab	00002035303	200	0
Darvon-N ASA Tab	00002035402	240	320
Darvocet-N 100 Tab	00002036303	0	100
Multicebrin Tablet	00002037102	50	50
Ephedrine Sulfate 25	00002062402	1000	1000

It is arranged in the order of NDC numbers, but you might also like to have it listed in alphabetical order by drug name. This report will assist you in your manual ordering, since it shows you the quantities dispensed during the month. The comparison to the previous month is an extra feature to help you detect trends in usage. If you've been thinking to yourself, "Sure seems like the doctors are prescribing a lot more Darvon these days," you can verify your impressions from this report. You might like the comparison to extend even further back, say with the same month last year or with the average of the last 12 months. If you're going to get that thorough, you might want the report in order of percentage change, with the greatest changes in quantity at the head of the list. But that leads to our last method.

A Hot List. Perhaps your experience is that the only prescription drugs you're really in danger of running out of are the ones that are moving the fastest. The simplest inventory tracking method is just a list of the top 100 medicines over a given period of time. That's extremely easy for the computer to generate.

The final step in any method of inventory control is the placing of orders to replenish your stock. I mentioned briefly at the start of the chapter that electronic submission of orders is becoming common. Some wholesalers will provide you with small handheld devices which look like bulky calculators but which are, in fact, battery-powered computers. They are designed to let you count the stock on your shelves quickly and enter the numbers onto a small calculator-like keypad. They have sufficient internal memory to let you count your entire stock. After your count, you simply dial the wholesaler's special telephone number and connect the device. Your order will automatically be transmitted to bring your inventory back to your preselected levels. This capability is tailor-made for marriage to your data management system. A computer can easily place that phone call for you and transmit your orders. No doubt, this feature will be enhanced considerably in the future.

SUMMARY

Pharmacies are likely to be widely computerized during the next few years. Most are already using fairly sophisticated schemes and devices for product coding, billing, and electronic ordering. Computers can pay for themselves by the labor they save in form handling alone. Inventory control is the second primary benefit. The icing on the cake—the benefits that are next to impossible to achieve manually but which come almost free with a computer—are patient profiles and the related capability to catch adverse drug interactions.

Accounts receivable control is not a primary benefit. Most pharmacies' receivables are essentially a list of the outstanding claims to third-party plans. But a good data manager can help you fill out all those claim forms, keep track of rejected and otherwise confused submissions, and tell you which plans (if any) are profitable.

Notes

1. Jim Jackson, "The Microcomputer in a Pharmacy," in *Interface Age*, March 1983.

2. "Safety Prompts Computer Use in Drugstores" by Paul A. Engelmayer, in the *Wall Street Journal* of September 28, 1983, page 31.

3. Ibid.

4. A minor technical point: computers are highly accurate, but they have been known to make mistakes in copying information. The simple databases I described will go through at least two copying operations: once at the distributor, and again by the assembler of your computer system. The latter step may involve merging the information into a larger database, along with prices and other information. So in the final product, in the system sitting in your establishment, there has to be a way to verify that the numbers were all copied without error. This isn't particularly hard to do; there are several methods of adding up all the numbers to arrive at various kinds of sums which can be compared against the official sums. It's just the kind of thing that has to be provided, once we admit to any kind of responsibility for another person's welfare.

5. If you owned an imaginary store, you might even decide to violate the first objective occasionally—to let yourself run out of an item. That might be the right choice if the item is extremely expensive to stock (because of high cost per item or high perishability), or if you have no idea how well a new item will sell. But we'll stick to the objective for a pharmacy, at least for drugs, because a customer might become extremely anxious if you're unable to fill a needed prescription. And unlike a manufacturing firm, in a pharmacy you don't have the luxury of "back orders;" that is, telling customers to wait a few weeks until you can fill their prescriptions.

6. That "in theory" qualifier is a big one—it means in the absence of shoplifting, errors, and forgetting to tell the computer about the crates of spoiled tomatoes you threw away. Even with a computerized perpetual inventory, you'll still have to count your stock by hand every once in a while. But the once in a while will be a lot less often, and you'll have a more accurate guess at your stock levels in the meantime than with manual methods.

7. Automating your inventory is a must if you want to automate your general ledger as well, because inventory is a large part of your total assets. But before you can place a dollar value on your inventory, you'll have to decide how to judge the value of items in the face of ever-changing costs. You can decide to value every item at its replacement cost (the most recent cost); that's known as the Last-In-First-Out or LIFO valuation method. Or, you can use the original cost of each item when you bought it, which is the First-In-First-Out or FIFO method. As a compromise, you can take the Weighted Average cost—the total cost of the entire stock of any one item, divided by the number of pieces. You have to decide that not only so you can estimate your total assets, but also so you can judge your profits and losses in dollars and cents for your tax return. Obviously this is not a decision to be made lightly, especially since the IRS won't let you change your mind whenever you feel like it.

8. If your computer is handling your accounts payable and cash disbursements as well, the ordering process can be made highly automatic. It can print the orders and post the amounts you owe for the purchase to your accounts payable, or else print the checks if an advance payment is required. If you really want to get automated, find yourself a bank that allows electronic funds transfer, and drug distributors that allow submission of orders electronically over the phone (as was illustrated in the physicians' chapter). Then all of us humans can go fishing ....

Chapter 8

Okay, How Much?

In the preceding chapters we've been discussing the applications and potential benefits of data management in your office. By now you have some idea whether a computerized data manager would be helpful to you. Because you care about the business side of your profession, there is, no doubt, one major question still bothering you:

"How much?"

In this final chapter we will look at the investment required for a system that will support those applications we've been talking about. There is a wide range of costs in computers—from $100 on up into the millions. So, before we can arrive at a price, we have to briefly discuss the performance we'll require from the machinery.

People who have never worked with computers often have unrealistic speed expectations. If the computer takes ten seconds to retrieve the data on a particular client, they get worried. "What's it doing? I thought computers were supposed to be fast!" Never mind that it would have taken minutes to retrieve the information by hand. They expect to press a key and have an instantaneous answer.

That expectation is a universal human trait. If you were to install a doorbell in your house that could not be

**WHAT TO EXPECT
FOR PERFORMANCE**

ASHTON·TATE ■

heard by someone on the doorstep, your visitors would invariably push the button two or three times and then begin to knock. *Something* is supposed to happen. A good programmer is aware of that human trait, and always provides some immediate response to a command, even if it's only a message like "Please wait."

So let me first set a few limits on speed. To make the numbers specific, let's assume you want to see the historical information on a particular client. You would like to enter the client's name, not an arbitrary number, and have the computer display the rest of the data on the video screen. In the kind of system that I like to work with, this task takes an average of three seconds, from the time you finish typing in the name you want to see, to the time the complete record is displayed on the screen. The actual time depends upon how much information has been stored on each client and the total number of clients.

It sounds pretty fast compared to a filing cabinet, but the time adds up when you want to do something concerning *all* of your clients. The best example is a monthly billing. To prepare the bills, your data manager has to examine the records for each of your clients to find out which ones owe you money. Then, for each one with a positive balance, it has to do a few calculations and print the statement. If you are a dentist with 1000 active patients, and 300 of them need statements, then the information retrieval step will take three seconds per patient, times 1000 patients (all of them have to be checked), for a total of 3000 seconds or about one hour.

That doesn't include printing time. If each of the 300 statements requires 0.3 minutes for printing (the number we used in Chapter Three), that's an additional 90 minutes. The total job will take two and one-half hours, faster than manual typing, but definitely not instantaneous.

The two most important elements in this time estimate are the speed of the printer and the speed of the storage devices, the magnetic disks on which your files are recorded.[1] These two factors are much more important in the applications we're discussing than the ones described in a

ASHTON·TATE ■

sales brochure. Ignore the speed of the central processor and any other statistic calculated in units of megahertz or microseconds. Anything you can't measure on your wristwatch has little real meaning for your business. That advice may sound like heresy to some of you, but the central processor is not the bottleneck in most data management applications—disk and printer speeds are the most important considerations.

The printer in my time estimate was a "letter-quality" unit, one that will produce statements that appear to have come from a standard office typewriter. An alternative is a "dot matrix" printer, so-called because it forms characters out of many tiny dots. Examples of both styles are shown in Figure 1.

A letter-quality model that prints at 50 characters per second will cost from $2000 to $3000. A dot matrix model will print twice that fast, and cost only one third as much. If that appearance is acceptable, you can save money and gain speed. Thus, if a dot matrix is sufficient, the printing time of my example would be reduced to 45 minutes.

The time estimate of the storage devices in the example was based on the use of a high-speed disk, usually called a hard or fixed disk. An alternative is to use a lower-speed, lower-cost device called a floppy, flexible, or removable disk. For the same simple retrieval task with a floppy disk system, the average retrieval time rises to eight seconds. The look-up part of the monthly billing job will increase to 8000 seconds, an additional hour and 20 minutes.

Faster speed is not the only advantage of a hard disk. Typically, it will store from five to ten million characters, a capacity which is ten to 20 times greater than that of floppy disks. With that much room you can keep a large volume of information on hand at one time. The difference in ease of use is also greater than what you would expect by just comparing the numbers. You do not have to worry about making room on the disk for the storage of information on marginally active clients, at least not

ASHTON·TATE ■

nearly as often. You don't have to worry about whether you have room to save some new information or a new document.

My recommendation is to use a hard disk with the advantages of faster speed, greater storage capacity, and fewer "housekeeping" headaches. The extra $1000 to $2000 investment over the cost of a good floppy disk system is worth it. If you want to start with floppy disks to save money, at least until you get a feel for what can be done with a computer in your office, by all means do so. But be sure that the system you buy will accept a hard disk later, if and when you choose to add one.

WHAT TO EXPECT FOR COST

There is one major assumption in my cost estimates that must be clarified: Your business is small enough—less than about ten full-time employees—so that a small computer will handle your data management needs. As a very rough guideline, and a risky one given the rate at which prices change in this market, a small computer will cost under $15,000. That's not to say a larger machine, one that costs upwards of $20,000, might not be suitable for your business; it may very well be what you need if your business has more than ten income producers, or more than two or three stores you wish to view as an integrated whole. But we have to limit our discussion to some reasonable arena. The range of costs is wide enough even for the "smaller" computers.

The concept of "viewing as an integrated whole" is a key one. Large companies and large professional offices, with a good deal more than ten income producers, often use several small, relatively inexpensive computers. Large law firms are a good example. They might have dozens of personal computers (or word processors, which are pretty much the same thing) sitting on lawyers' and secretaries' desks. But those machines are usually intended to be paperwork-saving aids for one or a few workers. They are not expected to *manage* the data—the timekeeping and billing and receivables and financial reports—of the entire business.

ASHTON·TATE ■

This is a sample of the print from a "letter-quality" printer. It will produce statements that appear to have come from a standard office typewriter.

The alternative is called a" dot-matrix" printer. The name comes from the method of forming characters out of many tiny dots, as you can see by examining the letters. If this appearance is acceptable, you can save money and gain speed.

Figure 1. Comparison of letter-quality and dot-matrix printers

Finally, we're ready to discuss the investment needed for your computer—a computer small enough to be affordable by your business, but large enough to manage the data generated by that same thriving and profitable business as an integrated whole.

Class One: The Beetle. Even after limiting ourselves to small business computers, there's still a wide price range to explore. I find it helpful to view the range in three segments. At the low end of the price range is a computer with floppy disks and a moderate speed dot matrix printer. That combination will costs from $2500 to $3000. There are dozens of brand names and models of computers that fall into this class: Apple II, IBM PC, Radio Shack, just to name the most widely advertised. They are in the Volkswagon Beetle class: fine little machines, but not something you would use to haul furniture across the country.[2]

Because of the limited storage capacity of the disks, such a system will not handle a very large office. At least, it won't handle it for very long. Let's say you're using it as a dental office assistant, and you merely expect it to store your daily transactions—the procedures you perform each day. Each transaction will need roughly 50 characters of storage space. If your office performs 60 procedures a day, that's 3000 characters. Since an average floppy disk stores about 300,000 characters, you will be able to remember 100 days on a single disk.[3]

Maybe 100 days on a small, $5 floppy disk sounds pretty good to you. But what do you do if you want to look at a profitability report for an entire year? (Sure, there are ways to do it—for instance, by creating a condensed historical file of just the bottom-line figures for each month.) We haven't even allowed for your database of client names yet, that all-important client list we've been managing throughout the book. In fact, some of the applications we have analyzed, like third-party tracking and perpetual inventory control, won't begin to fit on a floppy disk-based machine.

Hence, I do not recommend a floppy disk-only system for professional data management. If you feel like buying one to get your feet wet, that's fine. The worst that can happen, if for some reason you can't later upgrade it for your full needs, is you will have it to use as a word processor, or as a learning machine for your children.

Class Two: The Station Wagon. A much more practical system for data management is one with a hard disk (ten million or more character storage) and either a fast letter-quality printer or a very fast dot matrix printer. The combination will cost from $4,000 to $8,500.

This the station wagon class, not necessarily any faster than a Beetle if you only want to carry one or two persons, but definitely more roomy. Some typical examples are the IBM XT, Kaypro 10, Televideo, and a host of IBM look-alikes (Eagle, Corona, Digital Equipment).

Class Three: The Mack Truck. At the extreme high end of our range are systems that are still based on essentially "small" computers, but are powerful enough to handle several users at one time. This is the kind of system you need, for example, if you're running a drugstore with four pharmacists, and you want all four to be able to use the same computer at the same time. All of them need access to the same large database of customer histories and drug prices. When pharmacist number one fills a prescription, you want the inventory database to reflect the change instantly. You don't want pharmacist number two to have to wait. Nor do you want him using his own separate and unconnected computer which doesn't know about the inventory depletion until much later.

The typical equipment in this class will include one or more large capacity hard disks (ten to 80 million characters of storage), two or more consoles for the multiple users, and two or more printers. A few brand names are Altos, CompuPro, and Televideo, although such a system might well be assembled from several different lines. Your investment for the hardware alone will vary from $9,000 to $15,000, or perhaps even more, with a direct correlation to the planned number of simultaneous users.

ASHTON·TATE ▪

Software is the sets of instructions which direct the machine to do what you want, much like the procedural outlines we've demonstrated throughout the book. It is purchased separately, and can vary just as widely in price as the hardware. The price range, however, is not due to speed and capacity, but rather to how well the software *fits* your individual business.

Buying and fitting software to your business is very much like buying clothes, a business suit if you will. Your cheapest alternative is to buy a suit off the rack. You can really save money if you buy it at a discount outlet that won't do any alterations. If you have a standard build, not too tall, both arms the same length, the suit may fit you just fine. The low price doesn't necessarily mean the suit is made from low-quality fabric. In software, that corresponds to buying a "canned" general-purpose package through the mail. If you work the same way everyone else does in your profession, the program "off the rack" may be just what you want.

If you're a little removed from average, you might be better served at a clothing store that will make free alterations. You'll pay a little more than you would at the discount store, but at least the coat won't ride up in the back. You will not, however, be able to have *major* adjustments made, and you won't have much room for complaint if you gain weight later on. This is equivalent to buying that same "canned" software package from a local computer store. You'll pay more, but the store will make minor alterations for you. Another advantage is the helpful advice you'll get while you're shopping; the store (you hope) will try to prevent you from buying something that really looks bad on you.

The third choice is what I call a customized suit. This is how I like to buy clothes, given my current economic state of affairs. I buy a good-quality suit that approximately fits, but decline the offer of alterations, even if they're free. I take the suit to my friendly tailor who fits it to me. He usually winds up redoing half the seams in the garment. I pay an extra 20 or 30 percent over the rack price, but the

ASHTON·TATE ■

result is almost as good as a true "custom-made" suit. If I gain weight (probable), or develop more powerful biceps (unlikely), I can go back to the same tailor for further alterations.

The most expensive approach is a totally tailor-made suit. You can choose the fabric, the color, and all the details. You can add watch pockets and monogrammed cuffs if you like. But you'll pay for it.

For most businesses I recommend the customized approach. Find a consultant. He will start with a good, basic package designed for your profession, and then tailor it to your particular needs. You can find one by talking to colleagues in your profession, looking in the yellow pages under "Data Processing Consultants," or by attending any professional conference or seminar with data processing topics on the agenda. The consultant's first service, after talking with you about your business, will be a demonstration of his recommended software package. That's something you definitely won't get if you order by mail and can't always get at a retail store. The demonstration does two things: it lets you make sure that the package actually runs and comes close to fitting you, and it shows you where you will need alterations. If you've been thinking about how your office does things, and outlining your manual methods, it will be obvious to you where a few seams have to be let out.

If you can't find a package that is close enough to be customized, only then should you consider a completely tailor-made program. Human hours are expensive. The same consultant who customized your software might be the one who will design the system for you. But his time, and therefore your expense, will be substantial. (Just as the same tailor is willing to adjust my suits or to make me one from scratch.)

How expensive? I've seen comprehensive programs for professionals advertised at less than $1,000 from mail-order outlets. The same package from a computer dealer might cost from $1,500 to $2,500. A consultant who will customize the program, install it in your office, and train your staff will charge you $3,000 to $9,000. But a specially written package starts from there and goes up as high as $20,000, sometimes even more. After all, what would *you* charge a client who wanted to monopolize your time for months?

Actually, I've omitted one option: You could write your own software. It would cost you only a few hundred dollars for a word processor and the programming language, the basic tools of the trade. But make a firm resolution at the outset never to multiply your normal hourly rate by the number of hours you will be putting in. It's like working on your own car when you really don't know very much about automobile mechanics. If you enjoy doing it, and you don't mind making mistakes while you're learning, or taking a longer time, then do it. Just don't pretend it's cheaper.[4]

THE BOTTOM LINE

Selecting a system with adequate capacity, and then finding software that fits your needs, are the difficult tasks for you or your consultant. After you've gotten that far, simple addition will give you your total investment. A Beetle with a suit off the rack (I knew these analogies would get out of hand sooner or later) might add up to only $3,500. A Mack truck in a tailor-made tuxedo could cost ten times that, but still be a good investment for you.

My recommendation for the average professional office lies between the two extremes—a station wagon with a customized suit. That's the example I'll use for the remainder of the chapter. The typical total is:

Computer with hard disk, good printer,
and miscellaneous cables and supplies:
$7,000 (plus or minus $2,000)
Software: $6,000 (plus or minus $3,000)
Total initial investment:
$13,000 (plus or minus $5,000)

Service. Notice that I said initial investment in that price list. Your system will need occasional maintenance, just as your car does. Even though the problems are often minor (the last two I remember were a loose screw and a kicked-

ASHTON·TATE ■

loose power plug), they still prevent the continuation of business as usual. Doing your own programming is one thing; repairing printers and disk drives is quite another.

The standard solution to this problem is a service contract. You pay a yearly fee to the dealer from whom you purchased the equipment, or to a third-party firm that specializes in computer service. That fee may include periodic preventive maintenance, such as a quarterly cleaning of your disk drives and printer, but more commonly it's only an insurance policy. If and when the system needs repair—major or minor—you can call the service company and expect them to fix it. There are variations on this theme from one company to the next, of course. Some will make house calls, others won't. A few will guarantee a maximum repair time of one business day.

The annual cost of a service contract will vary from six to 18 percent of the purchase price of the equipment. The exact amount depends primarily on the level of service promised. The 18 percent maximum should get you house calls and a guaranteed quick response time. In our example ($7,000 for hardware), we will use an average figure of 12 percent, making the cost of the service contract $840 per year.

COST JUSTIFICATION

The moment of truth: will a computerized data manager be profitable for your business? How soon will it start earning you money? Sooner than the new copy machine or extra secretary you're considering? In the business world, questions like these are answered objectively with a cost justification or payback analysis—a systematic way of comparing alternative investments on the basis of cold, hard profit.

This is not the only way to make the decision. You may have enough capital to buy the copy machine, hire a new secretary, and install a computer all at the same time. If you're doing that well, I'd honestly say your gut feeling will be a better guide than a numerical analysis. Or you may want a computer because all your colleagues have

ASHTON·TATE ■

one, and you're going on their experience. Those are all perfectly valid reasons.

A cost justification is called for if you have one or more of the following problems:

- •More than one investment is attractive, and you don't have enough free capital to do everything now.
- •You want to consult the opinions of your advisors or investors.
- •You need to convince a bank or other lending institution.

To show you how it's done, we'll start with a very simple cost justification based on a specific hypothetical case. A dental clinic that's already using an outside service bureau to handle monthly billing, collection chores, and other receivable matters is considering computerization. This simplifies the calculation because it allows us to represent the cost of billing as a single monthly charge. Here are the assumptions: The clinic has 600 active patients and a monthly total in receivables of $40,000. The outside billing service is charging $400 a month. Even though an in-house computer usually requires less work on the part of your staff, we'll assume that their labor is equivalent in both methods.

The typical experience of doctors or dentists who have used both an outside service and an in-office computer is that the computer speeds up the collection of receivables by about a month. The primary benefit of the computer, then, is the improvement in cash flow.

The faster cash flow is valued by calculating the interest that the same money would be drawing if you indeed had it that much sooner. Figuring an annual return of 12 percent, or one percent per month, then:

Benefits
$40,000 receivables, 1 percent x $40,000 = $400 per month one month sooner
Plus the saved expense of the outside service $400 per month, Total Benefits = $800 per month

Continuing Costs
    Supplies (paper, ribbons, disks)
                            $30 per month
    Service contract for computer
    ($840/year) $70 per month
           Total Costs = $100 per month
           Net Benefit = $700 per month

That's the figure that will offset your initial investment of $13,000 in the software and hardware. Ignoring taxes and inflation, you would regain your investment in a little over *18 months*, a very attractive payback period. Industrial companies generally strive for a payback period of less than three years.

For a slightly more complicated example, here's a cost justification for a pharmacy, using some of the benefits described in Chapter 7. We mentioned one store's experience that one less pharmacist was needed after computerization to handle the same workload, for a saving of about $20,000 per year. There was an additional labor saving in the elimination of overtime for the primary pharmacist; we'll take credit for one hour a day, and estimate his compensation at $25,000 a year.

The value of more accurate control over inventory can range up to 20 percent of the average assets being tied up in the inventory. For a pharmacy that's tracking only the prescription drugs, we'll assume only a five percent savings. An average-sized store might have a drug inventory worth $50,000, so the estimated benefit would be $2,500 per year.

We won't worry about the lesser benefits you might obtain by automating the payroll, accounts payable, or general ledger. We also won't try to put a value on improved customer relations. This will be a very conservative cost justification.

Benefits
    One less pharmacist, $20,000 salary
    saved $1,667 per month

ASHTON·TATE ■

1 hour/day of another's time (12% of
$25,000) $250 per month
Inventory control (5% of $50,000 =
$2,500 year) $208 per month
        Total Benefits = $ 2,125 per month

Continuing Costs
    Supplies (paper, ribbons, disks)
                              $30 per month
    Service contract for computer
    ($840/year) $70 per month
        Total Costs = $100 per month
            Net Benefit = $2,025 per month

If the investment is still $13,000, the payback period is only about *six months!*

Neither of these examples is very sophisticated. Each one calculates a simple linear payback, i.e., the value of money is constant. They don't recognize that a dollar today is worth more than one you'll save a few years from now. They don't count tax credits for the investment, even though the current tax laws offer sizeable incentives for this kind of investment. They don't estimate the true after-tax cost of the expenses (service bureau, accountant, and supplies). If you want to weigh all of these factors, you or your accountant can perform a discounted cash flow analysis, which tries to estimate the real difference in spendable cash due to an investment. That might be useful if you wanted to compare dissimilar types of investments, say a computer versus a non-business investment like municipal bonds.

If you are going to perform a cost justification, select a simple method and use it for purposes of comparison, like the miles-per-gallon rating of a car. An analysis of greater depth is not only beyond the scope of this book, but I do not believe that it is particularly important to your decision. There are too many factors that aren't easily quantified. An investment in your business has the potential to generate *more* business; municipal bonds don't. How do you judge that value? What if you were threatened with *losing* business because you didn't have a computer or a new diagnostic tool?

This situation occurs in the manufacturing industries, when a new process becomes widespread enough so that installing it is essential just to avoid losing a share of the market—*even when* the analysis predicted it would be a *drain* on cash flow! Without it, the plant's customers would go elsewhere, where they would receive better quality for less. I believe a similar phenomenon will occur in professional offices over the next few years. Clients will patronize the professionals who can give them timely, itemized bills, who can process the insurance claims quickly, who can advise them of new developments, or the danger of an adverse reaction. You will need data management just to remain competitive.

The philosophy at the heart of our discussion has been: Think About Your Business First. If you've analyzed even a few of your more important office procedures, and given some thought to what questions you will want answered a year from now, you've made an excellent start.

The second step should be to find a consultant or a dealer who shows some sincere interest in your business. Let the consultant take over the results of your analysis and the headaches—*you* do not have to become a computer expert. The time required for you to investigate all the software packages and design your own system would be prohibitive and self-defeating. The whole purpose of this book is to save your time and money.

SELECTING YOUR SYSTEM

Notes

1. Before I get letters from the technical types among you, let me clarify that the storage device is properly called the disk *drive*. The disk itself is really only the flat magnetic platter on which the information is stored. The disk is like a phonograph record. The drive is the turntable.

2. The automobile analogy is a good one to illustrate the difficulty of judging real performance from technical specs. The number of cylinders in the engine corresponds to the number of bits in the processor. More cylinders usually means more speed, but not necessarily. The displacement in cubic centimeters corresponds to the memory capacity in the computer. More displacement usually means more power, but not necessarily. The potential for greater speed and power can be nullified by an inefficient "slushomatic" transmis-

sion, or in a computer by inefficient software. Keep that in mind as we're discussing how to select a computer.

3. Such systems almost always have two floppy disk units, but don't be tempted to use that full double capacity in your calculations. Your software (the operating system, language, and application programs) has to be remembered somewhere! It will easily fill the first of those two disks.

4. A little clarification is in order concerning the three different classifications of software. The first kind of software your computer must have is an "operating system." This is a set of instructions that organizes the information you've entered and stores it on the magnetic disks in an orderly and easily retrievable fashion. The operating systems you're most likely to encounter go by the names of CP/M, MS-DOS, PC-DOS, and Unix.

The second piece of software your system needs is a "programming language." Examples are BASIC, FORTRAN, Pascal, or the more specialized data-management languages like dBASE II, FMS-80®, or R:Base®. These languages make it easy for you, or the designer of your system, to give the computer instructions, by letting you use vaguely English-like equations (such as PRICE = COST + FEE) and commands (such as PRINT PRICE or FIND SMITH).

The sequence of such commands and equations that actually describes what you want accomplished—corresponding to our procedural outlines—is called the "application program." *This* is the software in my price estimates. The other two kinds of software are either included in your hardware purchase or are relatively inexpensive compared to application programs.

SURVEY

Thank you for purchasing <u>Data Management for Professionals</u>.

Our readers are important to us. Please take a few moments to provide us with some information, so we can better serve you.

Once we receive your reader survey card, your name will be kept on file for mailings regarding future Ashton-Tate publications.

Name: _____

Company Name: _____

Address: _____

City/State: _____ Zip Code: _____

Country: _____ Date: _____

1) How did you first learn about this publication?
- 21-1 ( ) Someone who saw or bought it
- -2 ( ) Software dealer or salesperson
- -3 ( ) Hardware dealer or salesperson
- -4 ( ) Advertising
- -5 ( ) Published review
- -6 ( ) Computer store display
- -7 ( ) Computer show
- -8 ( ) Book store
- -9 ( ) Directly from Ashton-Tate

2) Where did you purchase this publication?
- 22-1 ( ) Directly from Ashton-Tate™
- -2 ( ) From my dBASE II® Dealer
- -3 ( ) Computer show
- -4 ( ) Book store

3) Have you purchased other Ashton-Tate products?
- 23-1 ( ) Yes   -23-2 ( ) No

If Yes, please check which ones:
- 23-3 ( ) dBASE II®
- -4 ( ) Friday!™
- -5 ( ) dBASE II RunTime™
- -6 ( ) dNEWS™
- -7 ( ) *Through the MicroMaze*
- -8 ( ) *Everyman's Database Primer*
- -9 ( ) *Reference Encyclopedia for the IBM® Personal Computer*

4) What type of software programs are you using now?
- 24-1 ( ) Accounting
- -2 ( ) Sales
- -3 ( ) Word Processing
- -4 ( ) Other (Please specify)_____
_____

5) What type of information-management software programs are you interested in?
- 25-1 ( ) Academic/Scientific
- -2 ( ) Agriculture
- -3 ( ) Building
- -4 ( ) Business
- -5 ( ) Financial
- -6 ( ) Health Care
- -7 ( ) Home/Hobby
- -8 ( ) Insurance
- -9 ( ) Membership/Registry
- -10 ( ) Professional
- -11 ( ) Real Property
- -12 ( ) Software Utilities

6) What software do you expect to purchase from this catalog?
- 26-1 _____
_____

7) Who are you purchasing the software for?
- 27-1 ( ) Business
- -2 ( ) Self

8a) Who will be the actual user of the software?
- 28-1 ( ) I will be
- -2 ( ) Someone else will be

Title: _____

8b) What make and model computer do you use?
- 28-3 _____

9) Do you expect to purchase any other software programs during the next 12 months? If so, what type?
- 29-1 ( ) Accounting
- -2 ( ) Sales
- -3 ( ) Inventory
- -4 ( ) Other (Please specify)_____

10) What software programs would you like to see developed?
- 30-1 _____
_____
_____

11) How can we improve this catalog?
- 31-1 _____
_____
_____

12) What is your primary business?

A. Computer Industry
- 32-1 ( ) Manufacturing
- -2 ( ) Systems house
- -3 ( ) DP supply house
- -4 ( ) Software
- -5 ( ) Retailing
- -6 ( ) Other _____

B. Non-Computer Business
- 33-1 ( ) Manufacturing
- -2 ( ) Retail trade
- -3 ( ) Wholesale trade
- -4 ( ) Financial, banking
- -5 ( ) Real estate, insurance
- -6 ( ) Engineering
- -7 ( ) Government
- -8 ( ) Education

- 34-1 ( ) Military
- -2 ( ) Health services
- -3 ( ) Legal services
- -4 ( ) Transportation
- -5 ( ) Utilities
- -6 ( ) Communications
- -7 ( ) Arts, music, film
- -8 ( ) Other _____

13) What is your position and title? Please check one in each list.

POSITION
- 35-1 ( ) Data processing
- -2 ( ) Engineering
- -3 ( ) Marketing/Advertising
- -4 ( ) Sales
- -5 ( ) Financial
- -6 ( ) Legal
- -7 ( ) Administration
- -8 ( ) Research
- -9 ( ) Operations/production
- -10 ( ) Distribution
- -11 ( ) Education
- -12 ( ) Other _____

TITLE
- 35-13 ( ) Owner
- -14 ( ) Chairperson
- -15 ( ) President
- -16 ( ) Vice President
- -17 ( ) Director
- -18 ( ) Manager
- -19 ( ) Dept. head
- -20 ( ) Independent contractor
- -21 ( ) Scientist
- -22 ( ) Programmer
- -23 ( ) Assistant
- -24 ( ) Other _____

14) How many employees are in your company?
- 36-1 ( ) Less than 10
- -2 ( ) 10 to 25
- -3 ( ) 26 to 100
- -4 ( ) 101 to 300
- -5 ( ) 301 to 1,000
- -6 ( ) over 1,000

15) I would like to remain on your mailing list.
- 37-1 ( ) Yes   37-2 ( ) No

- 38-1 I'd like to purchase additional copies of the current edition of *Application Junction* at $19.95.
- ☐ My check is enclosed.
My MasterCard/Visa card number is:

_____

Expiration date _____

Signature of cardholder _____

BUSINESS REPLY MAIL

FIRST CLASS   PERMIT NO. 959   CULVER CITY, CA

POSTAGE WILL BE PAID BY ADDRESSEE

ASHTON·TATE ™

10150 WEST JEFFERSON BOULEVARD
CULVER CITY, CALIFORNIA 90230